DOWN HOME
A JOURNEY INTO RURAL CANADA

WILLIAM DeKAY

Foreword by Neil Young

Toronto • New York

Stoddart

Published in 1997 by
Stoddart Publishing Co. Limited
30 Lesmill Road, Toronto, Canada M3B 2T6
Tel. (416) 445-3333   Fax (416) 445-5967
e-mail: Customer.Service@ccmailgw.genpub.com

Distributed in Canada by
General Distribution Services Inc.
30 Lesmill Road, Toronto, Canada M3B 2T6
Tel. (416) 445-3333   Fax (416) 445-5967
e-mail: Customer.Service@ccmailgw.genpub.com

Distributed in the United States by
General Distribution Services Inc.
85 River Rock Drive, Suite 202, Buffalo, New York 14207
Toll-free Tel.1-800-805-1083   Toll-free Fax 1-800-481-6207
e-mail: gdsinc@genpub.com

01 00 99 98 97   1 2 3 4 5

Cataloguing in Publication Data is available
from the National Library of Canada.

ISBN 0-7737-3039-7

Designed by Andrew Smith
Page composition: Andrew Smith Graphics Inc.
Map: Dorothy Siemens

Printed and bound in Hong Kong

*We acknowledge the Canada Council for the Arts and the Ontario Arts Council
for their support of our publishing program.*

Opening photographs:
The author's home on wheels, near Atlin, British Columbia;
jet trail over a deserted house, Orion, Alberta; strollers in a foggy sunset, Bonavista, Newfoundland.

For my parents, Grace and Eldon DeKay

One teenager's after-school chore, New London, Prince Edward Island.

CONTENTS

Cleanup after Sunday dinner at the Payne family summer cabin in
Old House Rocks, Newfoundland.

DOWN HOME

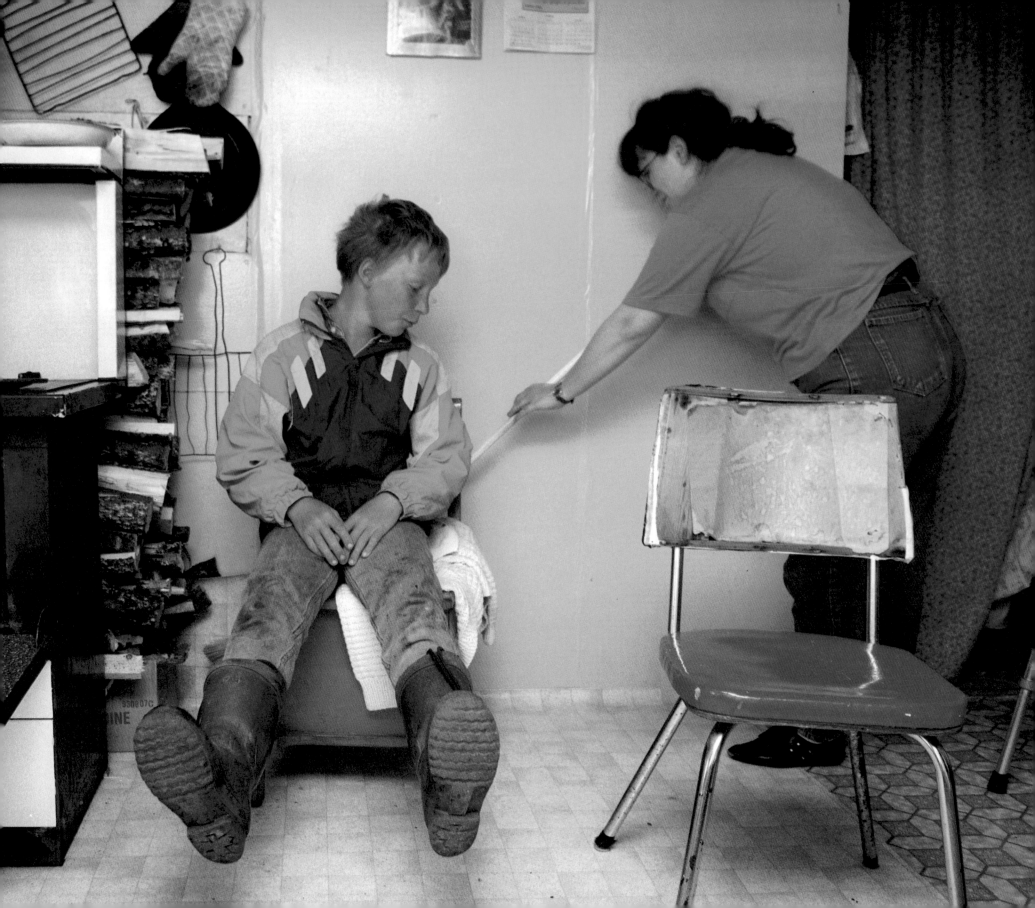

FOREWORD

by Neil Young

My hometown, Omemee, Ontario,
had a population of 750 when I was a boy.
We used to hunt turtles and fish for perch.

One day I was pulling a big snapping turtle
in my wagon down the sidewalk.
People were all watching me and saying, "Hi Neil!"

As I walked past Skinny Rehill's store,
I saw all the colours of the pansies in boxes,
hundreds of them, piled in rows along the sidewalk.
I was really a happy kid.

The photos in this book make me remember
my home, my roots, and my unique experience
as a young Canadian boy.

The old swimming hole, Renews, Newfoundland.

A family farm's next generation, Park Corner, Prince Edward Island.

ACKNOWLEDGEMENTS

With the the world's second largest country as my visual palette, I couldn't do it alone. The people I want to thank are numerous and fall into several categories.

First, I salute my Group of Seven — the companies that agreed to sponsor my dream.

Kodak Canada provided me with a generous supply of professional Ektapress and Royal Gold film. Every roll was processed, printed, and stored by SCL Imaging Group in Toronto.

Chrysler Canada handed me the keys to a Dodge Dakota four-wheel-drive pickup truck that proved its mettle over the toughest routes and through the most extreme variations in temperature.

Leisure Trailer Sales of Tecumseh, Ontario, customized a camper for life on the road.

Canada Post Corporation provided a welcome and much-needed infusion of cash.

A smaller yet pivotal supplier was Jamie's Collision & Refinishing of Windsor, Ontario. Their tasteful detailing of the truck and camper, including treatments of the sponsors' corporate logos, made the vehicle look so stylish that it served as the ideal ice-breaker and door-opener everywhere I went.

DayMen Photo Marketing of Toronto wrapped me in Lowe Alpine outerwear, which provided great warmth and mobility during one of the most bitter winters on record. Rounding things out, they equipped me with the complete Mamiya 6 photographic system.

I couldn't have taken the first step on my journey without the contributions of these corporations. But certain individuals within these organizations are the people who made things happen, notably: Michael Mayzel and Uwe Mummenhoff of DayMen Photo Marketing; Ron Waters of Kodak Canada; Gary Baldwin of Chrysler Canada; Jamie Bolton of Jamie's Collision & Refinishing; Jim and Tom Raymond of Leisure Trailer Sales; Paul Perkins and Joe Angellotti of SCL Imaging Group; and Helen Mrakovics of Canada Post Corporation.

I am grateful for the efforts of Jack Stoddart and his team of first-rate professionals.

This book has Sandy White's creative touch. She brought her usual trademarks: abundant energy, organization, and the highest qualities of writing and editing — mixed together with a fine sense of humour.

The best of what's in this book came from hundreds of people willing to share their knowledge, give directions, and introduce a stranger to their friends and families. A list of all who extended the hospitality of their homes appears at the end of this book.

A number of people with whom I broke bread or stayed awhile also sustained me by sharing their philosophies of life or by listening to mine. When I think of them I see kindred spirits. They include, in the order we met: Richard Adams, Lucille Horrelt, Faye and Peter Vido, Dave Rex, Monique Tobin and Greg Locke, George Francis, Robert and Roslynn Wilby, Marichka and Mark Côté, Gary Boissineau, Burton Penner, Hannah Lin and John Farrell, Phil Gatensby and JoAnne Kelpi.

A long list of friends, family members, and advisers supported me in various ways: Tony Stikeman, Bill Platten, Hope Beverstein, Bob Dent, Alison Manzer, Arthur Gelgoot, the DeKay family, Gary High, Paul Gero, Rich Clarkson, Tom Kennedy, Randy Miller, Mike Smith, Larry Levin, Rick Smolan, Nick and Jane Harris, David McKay, Rob Musial, Nicholas DeGrazia, Ron and Isabel Nelson, Rob and Lisa Nelson, John and Mary Stikeman, Jamie Stikeman, Duncan Graham, Pam Roddy and Bob Atkinson, Sue McKee and Eric Boyes, Bev and Bob Thompson, Julie Candler and Alan Hayes, Mary and Bill Schoen, Jim Wedlake and family, Jay and Lisa Asquini, Bruce Horsburgh, Brad Thompson, Mary Anne Toperczer, Leila Lee, Shelley Bolton, Nancy Baldwin, Vito Froio, Rose Corno, Ron Benson, Paula Tite, Becky Hall, Delilah Capstick, Ursula Belaoussoff, Mike Fanning, Robert Boudreau, Dean Goodwin, Avard Woolaver, and Grant Fairley.

Finally, a thank-you does not begin to show enough appreciation for Paula, who put her own dreams on hold so I could realize mine.

WILLIAM DEKAY
HARROW, ONTARIO

Old-timer Francis Powers, Brigus South, Newfoundland.

Aspens line an old mountain road near Kelly Lake, British Columbia.

THE JOURNEY DOWN HOME

The seeds of this journey took a long time to sprout. They were first planted among the corn and wheat fields of my family's southwestern Ontario farm, where I wandered as a teenager with my camera. I revelled in the changing seasons, and the farming activities associated with each. Once, my father and I stood watching as an old-timer harvested his crop using a vintage combine. "Better photograph these pioneers, Bill, before it's too late," he said.

The seeds took root a decade later, when I was standing in a bookstore. Its shelves were crowded with photographic tributes to Canada's natural wonders, our thriving urban centres, our diverse cultural and ethnic heritages. But the sort of book I wanted to do was conspicuous by its absence. Among the many hundreds of titles, not one celebrated the lives of "ordinary" Canadians in rural areas across the country. My father was right.

These were the people I was interested in — the ones I might have continued to live among, had I stayed on the land. From those early adventures with my camera, I knew my path would lead elsewhere, away from farming. I went to the United States, and lived and worked for eight years as a photojournalist. Over time, my curiosity drew me back; homesickness, too. I became restless to travel Canada, to photograph my changing country before it was too much changed.

When I began to look for corporate sponsorships, it soon became obvious that my quest was not universally applauded. (If a letter ends with the words "good luck," it's bad news.) At times, the reaction seemed to be that there wasn't all that much to be discovered in our own backyard. Many people felt this way. Once, while travelling through rural Quebec, I bumped into a swarm of press photographers, hot on the trail of a political figure. One of them asked me what I was doing there. When I explained, he said, "Why Canada?" Another photographer said that he too had gone all across the country, but that he'd been far more impressed with the landscapes than with the people, who seemed rather alike. My reaction was: What's wrong with that?

We're big on differences in this country, partly because we're just that — big. Even on a personal level, it's easy for Canadians to lose touch with one another; it's hard to get around. Elderly people told me about the grandchildren they never see. Their own kids had gone down the road, seldom if ever to return. This in itself poses a significant challenge to old-fashioned values, the simple joys that used to mark rural life. Vast distances also conspire against a unifying vision of who we are as a nation. Each region's commanding physical presence inspires passionate loyalties. But as I tried to thread together the themes of people, place, and identity, I realized that we are a nation of down-home patriots. When people say, as many did, "This is God's country," they mean their own slice of Canada.

That's why a journey to all points of the compass seemed the best, perhaps the only, way to come to grips with an otherwise ungraspable whole. I wanted to get over and behind the walls that have been solidified by regional interests or political concerns. Having done this, I see rural Canadians becoming more attached to one another — or, at the very least, more curious. They have more in common than they know. They are, more than they might realize, neighbours.

I achieved a great deal of freedom in my travels, because of the trusty camper truck. Life in my home on wheels had its ups and downs, but on balance it was the only way to go. And go I did, for eighteen months, 1993 to 1994, from the hilly lanes of Newfoundland to the unpaved fringe of the Northwest Territories. The weather, of course, was a prime factor. For roughly half the year, depending on where I was, I could work long days and set my own pace. But by late autumn, survival considerations took precedence over serendipity. I could make photographs outside for only a limited number of hours each day. As the light decreased, so did the number of people who were out and about and willing to talk to a stranger. The volume of invitations into homes declined as predictably as my camper's thermometer. I warmed myself with the concept that with all the tourists long gone, I had the whole country to myself.

Of course there were all sorts of momentary discomforts. It was tedious to worry about the everyday conveniences you take for granted in a home that's not in perpetual motion. At various times, I was hot, cold, bone weary, soaking wet, burned out, half-starved, and strapped for cash. I was lied to and insulted; twice I was shoved around. Once, somebody tried to sell me bad art — a carving that started out as a seal and ended up as a sabre-toothed something with glued-on tusks. But despite the rigours of travel, I miss the road.

For quite some time, I held out hopes of finding images that would depict the good old days — traditional approaches to life and work. But much of that is gone, at least on the surface. In Newfoundland, all-terrain vehicles have replaced horses, even if their owners are octogenarians. Out West, enormous tractors and combines seem to dwarf the land; the fields resemble agricultural factories. In backwoods Alberta, I met a man who was described as "the last of the mountain men," but even he deals with monthly electric bills. Of course, the old-time farmer I once watched with my dad had long since passed on.

At first, it was discouraging to realize that the images I was seeking had disappeared, for the most part. I lost count of the number of times someone said I should have been there a month, a year, even a week earlier to photograph some great old character, now dead. But then my eyes opened to the legacy of these pioneers: their pioneering spirit. The evidence was all around me, in the ways their children and grandchildren approach the challenges of their own lives. Times were hard for the pioneers, but people today don't have it all that easy either. One man told me the spirit of the prairies is the same as it was fifty years ago. Actually, that was true almost everywhere.

So I kept on going. I frequented towns so tiny that the churches shared preachers and the mayor doubled as a fireman. Everywhere I went, I was the stranger — possibly even a hot topic of local conversation. The business of explaining myself developed a rhythm with each repetition; the feeling of being a stranger became so familiar that I'd sometimes forget I was one. Few others did. Longtime inhabitants of rural areas often find that the community inhabits — and inhibits — them. Outwardly, toward each other, they're all smiles and hi-how-are-you. Inside, they harbour secrets, some of which they divulged to me. I heard a lot of brutal gossip and harsh prejudices, along with deep, otherwise unspoken longings. (No one need worry; it all went out the other ear.)

On the other hand, the fact that everybody knew everybody else for miles around was, for me, an advantage. I was handed along like a chain letter, pointed in what people felt might be fruitful directions. Even with their help, though, I may have set the Canadian record for U-turns. Every day, I made at least two or three. The optimum speed to drive and still absorb the passing scene, I discovered, is 50 kilometres per hour. Any faster, and I'd miss things. Many mornings I would look at the map, and decide which direction to head in, based on the most intriguing place-name. (Here, rural Canada is abundantly well-to-do. Our forefathers' sense of humour can be seen in a glance at a map.) This provided a focus for the day, but it didn't mean that I'd get there in a straight line — or, if I got there at all, that I'd stay for long.

What began as a voyage to document the lives of others became, in time, an equal passage within. The journey was both healing and spiritual. As I went along, I began to ponder less and trust my intuition more, while keeping my wits about me and the goal in sight. In many respects, this book is the result of getting up each day, not knowing what I was going to find, but trusting that I'd know it when I found it, and be ready to make something of it. Sometimes you have to put your faith in what you cannot see.

I took along three books. One was *The Americans,* the visionary 1950s photographic documentary by Robert Frank. By chance and good luck, we met at his home on Cape Breton Island. The second was *Blue Highways,* by William Least Heat-Moon. The third was John Steinbeck's classic *Travels with Charley.* One quote from Steinbeck must suffice: "We find after years of struggle that we do not take a trip; a trip takes us. In this a journey is like a marriage. The certain way to be wrong is to think to control it." This is advice to take anywhere, even if you're not travelling.

This book is about the kind of people who open their doors to a stranger with the offer of a home-cooked meal, a bed, or a shower. Behind the ones who appear in these pages are hundreds like them: the woman who patched my worn-out jeans; the man who crafted a film storage cabinet for my camper; the child whose crayon poster graced my refrigerator door; the husband-and-wife trappers who gave me the top bunk on a winter's night; and the Inuit family who shared their tent next to the Beaufort Sea.

This book is about a journey enriched by many firsts and a few lasts: my first Native sweat lodge ceremony; my first time on a dogsled, on snowshoes, on a trapline; my first whale hunt, spring trail ride, fall roundup, and powwow; my first taste of moose, caribou, muktuk, and beaver. It's about checking lobster traps at sunrise on a crisp spring day and watching the northern lights dance their magic on a cold winter night. It's about witnessing a community's grief and the precariousness of living close to nature in all its beauty and cruelty. It's about reaping what you sow, be it a crop or an idea planted long ago.

My experiences do not make me an authority on Canada. I simply hope to give some feel for the land and its people and to share some of the rewards and wisdom that come from such a journey. The best explanation of my quest was offered by someone I met. She said I made the trip to iron out the wrinkles in my soul.

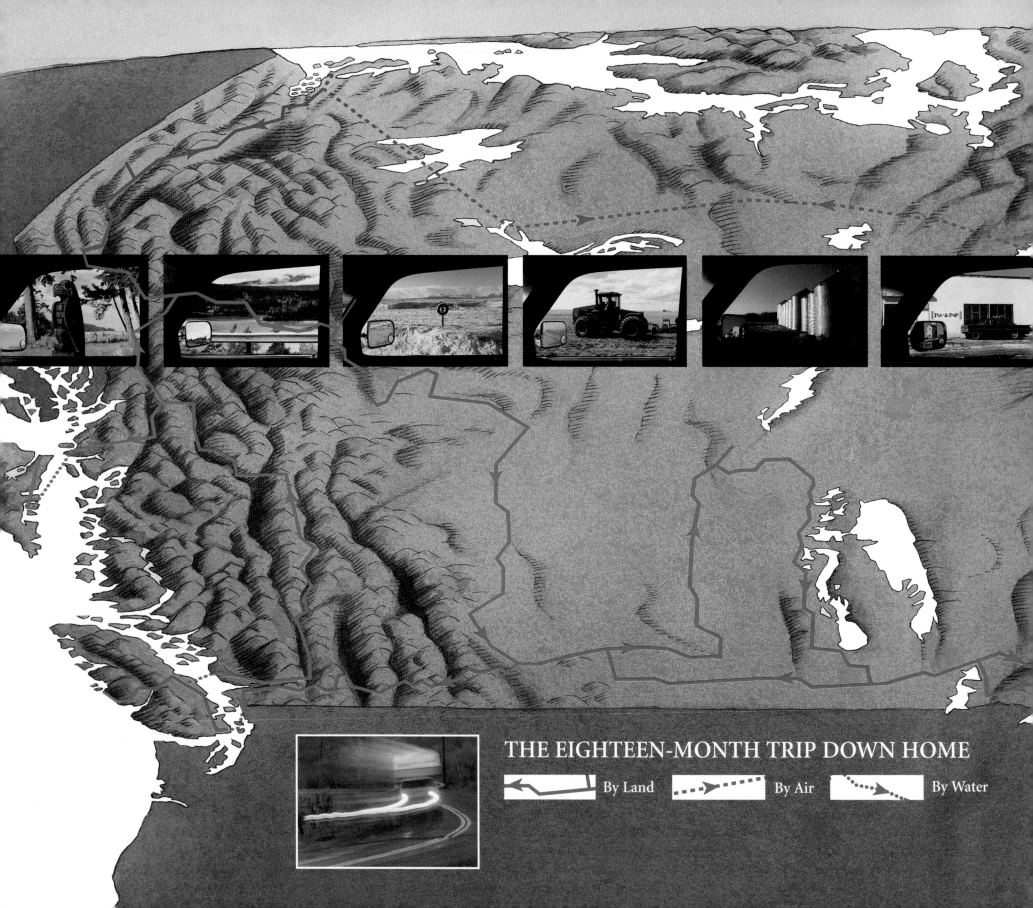

THE EIGHTEEN-MONTH TRIP DOWN HOME

By Land   By Air   By Water

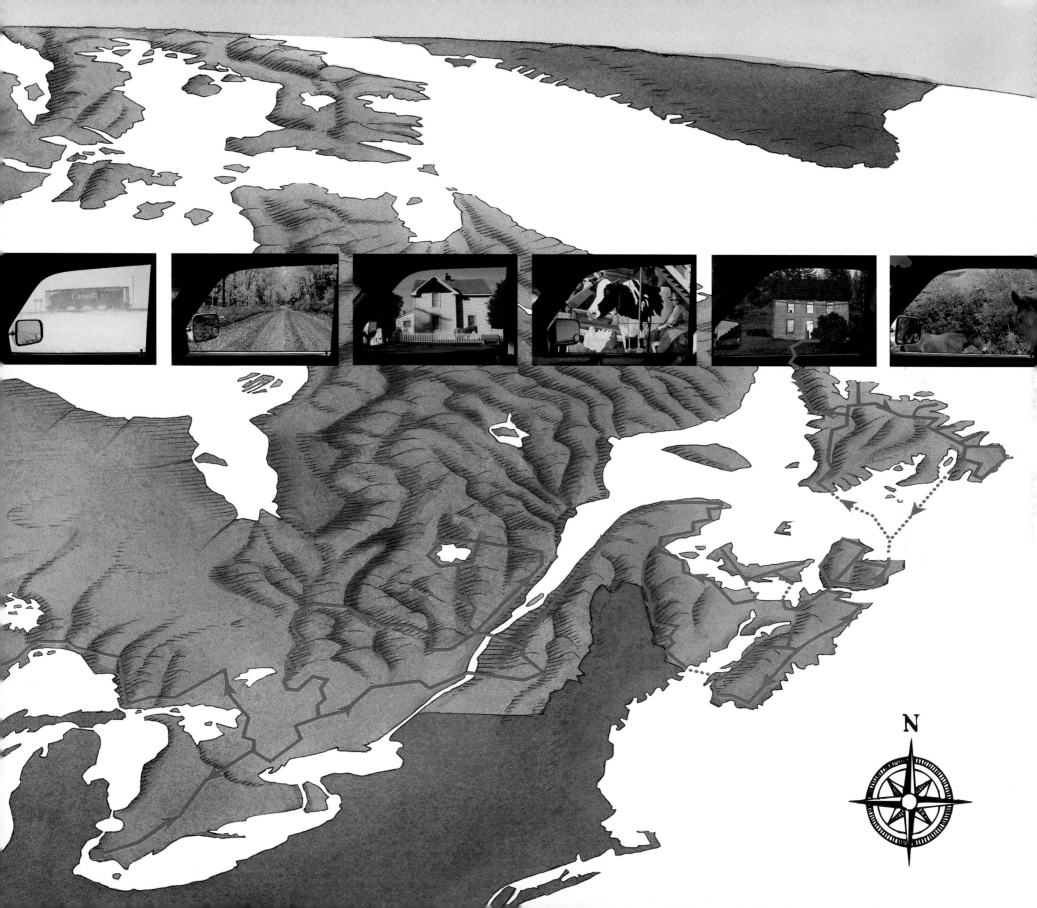

HORWOOD, NEWFOUNDLAND
"Since I was big enough to sew, I've been making quilts," said Bessie Hodder as
she held one of her latest creations, fresh from the clothesline.

HOME

I must have been in a couple of hundred kitchens across Canada. I can find my way around. Glasses are to the right of the sink; so is the cutlery drawer. Trash, if it's under the sink, is on the left. Many people call their lunch "dinner" and their dinner, "supper." Bacon and scrambled eggs — just like my mother's — is the breakfast most often served to company. Brunch does not exist.

Most of my mealtime invitations were spur of the moment; people didn't have the chance to clean up or impress a guest. Here's my report on Canadian housekeeping: overall, excellent, but seldom spic-and-span. Often cluttered, but usually organized. Meals are taken at the kitchen table, often with the TV going. Dining room tables have their place — as a household filing system.

Every offer of a home-cooked meal (or, especially, a shower) was eagerly accepted, but my home on wheels afforded comfort and self-sufficiency, albeit in miniature. The living space measured six-by-five and six feet high, plus a berth over the cab. My refrigerator had a six-inch freezer; my TV, a six-inch screen. I became proficient at opening tins and at making infinite variations on spaghetti. A favourite meal was take-out roasted chicken, augmented by my own boiled potatoes and vegetables.

I avoided motels and commercial campgrounds for three reasons: they weren't in my budget; most places I went were too small to have them; and I wanted to meet the local folk, not fellow travellers.

In good weather I parked undisturbed along the sea, on riverbanks, or in open fields. With permission, I'd park on private property, at shopping centres, or truck stops. I slept outside bingo halls (with the sound of N-7 and B-13 echoing in my dreams) and beneath lighthouses (foghorns are loud enough to wake the dead).

On winter nights I'd find an electrical outlet to plug in my life-support systems. A propane furnace and two fans prevented my water supply from freezing solid. State-of-the-art clothing and a mummy sleeping bag did the same for me. Keeping the water tanks and lines from freezing proved to be a major daytime challenge, too. As I drove, minus 10 degrees Celsius quickly became minus 40 inside the camper. The john stayed frost-free if I replaced the water with windshield washer fluid, but I finally had to drain the tanks and lines. Jugs of drinking water rode in the cab with me. I brushed my teeth in restaurant washrooms.

In addition to the prospect of a hot shower and good cooking, the best part of staying at people's homes was sharing moments in their lives. But I took to heart an old Maritimes saying: "Guests are like fish. After three days, they begin to smell."

TRINITY, NEWFOUNDLAND
George Ivany likes to keep his 1979 pickup truck looking good. This is a yearly ritual. He told me it doesn't make sense to pay $900 for one of those city paint jobs, when the body is just going to rust out again in the salty air.

LOURDES, NEWFOUNDLAND
Howard Hinks looks seaward as the wind dries both laundry and codfish. This is his private catch, which constitutes a fair bit of his winter food supply.

Peter and Faye Vido's philosophy is that they aren't living off the land, but in harmony with it. Twenty years ago they came to this remote part of New Brunswick and have since achieved almost total self-sufficiency.

Nothing is wasted. Today I watched Peter decapitate a calf that Faye had skinned. He split its skull with an axe — then, with a long-bladed knife, scooped out the brains to use in tanning. Their 200 acres are also home to horses, donkeys, goats, sheep, chickens, and geese. The lovingly tended garden yields vegetables and herbs.

It's a simple life, but rich in many ways. Before each meal, the family holds hands during a short prayer. After the noon meal, Peter takes a brief siesta. "An hour of sleep in the afternoon gives me three at night," he said. And just as well: he reads literature deep into the small hours.

This evening we walked to the edge of the treeline and lit a fire. Faye read the children a chapter from *The Education of Little Tree*. Songs were sung, and we paused on our way back down the hillside to admire the northern lights as they formed streaks of bright silver in the starry sky.

LOWER KINTORE,
NEW BRUNSWICK
The Vido family takes a break for the noonday meal around a homemade table in their two-room log home. But chores are always on the menu. Below, Faye leads by example, planting vegetable seeds while carrying a teddy bear belonging to her daughter Fairlight, so named because she was born at dawn.

MIDDLE OHIO, NOVA SCOTIA
While searching for another family
who lived off the beaten track, I
stopped to ask directions at the home
of Douglas and Geraldine Siegel. As I
knocked at the side door, their
granddaughter Megan was reading a
book in her favourite place.

CAP-AUX-RETS, QUEBEC
Marichka and Mark Côté embrace
in their living room.

FOGO ISLAND, NEWFOUNDLAND
Friends came and went while Jason
Penney jammed in the backyard.
Undaunted by two missing strings, he
was riveted on the endless repetition
of several bars from a song by his
favourite group, Guns N' Roses. A
school dropout, Jason dreams of
someday joining or starting a band.

LETHBRIDGE, ALBERTA
Pete Markus counts his blessings,
having spent most of the day
beating down a threatening grass
fire. He'd started it himself, as a
controlled burn, but it soon got out
of hand. The wind rose, blowing
sparks toward the house. Twice,
Pete asked me to fetch water from a
nearby canal. Pete collects Old West
memorabilia — everything from
vintage chuckwagons to what
seemed like hundreds of
mismatched wheels and
miscellaneous odds and ends. His
sister, Hilda Millard, said, "I call
this Clutter's Last Stand." Pete
sighed, patted his dog, Shadow, and
opened up a beer.

MOON LAKE, ONTARIO
Gary Boissineau built this one-room outpost cabin several years ago, when he established his first trapline. Pots, pans, bedrolls, and food hang out of reach of hungry wildlife. "What separates people from each other are walls," he told me. "Letting down the walls is how people become closer."

BOW CROW FOREST, ALBERTA
For mountain man Stanley Fisher, the hills are home and his best friend is his horse, Red Wing. Asked his age, he said, "I'm as old as my nose and my two big toes."

VERMILION BAY, ONTARIO
Home from three days on his trapline, Burton Penner attends to his son Forrest's bathtime. Burton earns most of his living by acting as a guide for adventure-minded tourists. His wife, Carlyn, came to Canada as a nanny from her native Philippines, and has mastered bannock, moose chili, roast beaver, and other staples of north-country cuisine.

GLACE BAY, NOVA SCOTIA
Glayan (Woody) Wujcik spends a quiet moment with his son Andrew. Like his father before him, Woody works in the Phalen Colliery in North Sydney. Pit closures and staff cuts have threatened the coal mining industry, but perhaps Andrew may someday follow in his family's footsteps.

BANKEND, SASKATCHEWAN
The queen of the barnyard pronounces an end to afternoon chores. Bob Blight's homestead is one of the province's dwindling number of fourth-generation family farms.

STANBRIDGE EAST, QUEBEC
Geneviève Baker plays her recorder after Easter dinner.

After his daughter, Tonya, and son, Trevor, caught the school bus, Robert Pelley and I talked at the kitchen table. Robert and Elizabeth made me feel welcome in their home. I didn't feel as if I were walking on eggshells, as I sometimes did during my seven years in Detroit, Michigan, where the frustration and hostility of blacks were often apparent. Racism cuts both ways and wounds us all.

Robert talked about his family's experiences with racial discrimination. "I've been called this and that on the streets in Halifax. I just keep walking. A few years ago, I might have stopped and fought. My mother always said to me, 'Do right to others that do wrong to you.' So I pay these comments no mind.

"But it doesn't stop, either. Trevor plays junior-league baseball; I go with him to tournaments around the province. Just the other weekend, we were in Afton, and Trevor heard this guy saying, 'Let's go get these niggers,' when our team took the field. This is what our children hear all the time. This is what the white kids hear from their parents. Now, if I have a racist attitude, then when you're around me, the children are going to pick up on it. That's why it's hard to say if it will ever end."

SUNNYVILLE, NOVA SCOTIA
Tonya Pelley psyches herself up before her mother, Elizabeth, gently applies ointment to a cut toe.

"You think this rain will stop the rhubarb?" asked Kim Smith.

"Nothing stops rhubarb," I replied.

It had rained all night, and still the downpour continued. I made photos of Kim as he rocked in a chair in the corner of his workroom. I said that the chair must be a good place to think.

"The chair's for sleeping," he said. "I do my thinking in bed."

ROCKY HARBOUR,
NEWFOUNDLAND
Phillip Piercey sits atop one of his father Frank's old lobster pots, which he sells to tourists as decorative items. Last summer he sold seven. The passing trade this particular evening was slow.

FRENCH RIVER,
PRINCE EDWARD ISLAND
A cottage porch, silhouetted against the Gulf of St. Lawrence.

WHITEHORSE, YUKON
Akalena Staruch and her mother
Laurie Jonasson cuddle while Caber,
the English sheepdog, stands guard.

BANKEND, SASKATCHEWAN
Their afternoon chores completed,
Bob Blight and his son Gene relax
with a cup of instant coffee.

TANCOOK ISLAND, NOVA SCOTIA
Percy Langille tills his backyard
garden before planting this year's
potato crop.

Evelyn Langille warned me that supper would be plain and simple. It turned out to be fresh-caught lobster and mackerel, boiled potatoes, carrots, pickled beets, and apple crisp. Every day, their cat, Sooty, receives a whole lobster of its own.

Percy's wake-up knock the next day came at 5 a.m. Fifteen minutes later, I was fully dressed, but only half-conscious. When I got downstairs to the kitchen, Percy was waiting in a rocking chair. He sounded impatient. "The light's getting on," he said. "You've got to dress quicker."

Percy had seventy-five traps to tend, but he's semi-retired now. He used to haul 250, all by hand. He could have given up his Class B fishing licence years ago, and slept in every morning. But here we were, out on the icy-cold Atlantic. At least there was very little wind; Percy said this was the best weather he'd seen all season.

I watched as he emptied, cleaned, and baited the traps with strong, sure motions. I asked if I could haul one, and found that it was much more difficult than he'd made it seem.

The lobsters began to stack up at our feet. One of them got a grip on my boots — a brand-new pair I'd borrowed from Evelyn. Its powerful claws left small indentations, but didn't puncture the rubber. We took twenty-two in all — one trap out of three, a respectable catch — but threw five back because they were too small. Percy explained that checking into the government wharf with an undersized lobster was a good way to lose your licence fast.

BRIGUS SOUTH, NEWFOUNDLAND
Francis Powers uses an all-terrain
vehicle to get around, but still keeps
a horse. He cuts hay with a scythe
and rakes it by hand.

ESKASONI, CAPE BRETON,
NOVA SCOTIA
Amidst the happy chaos of food,
friends, and family, Desiree
Sylliboy remains composed
during her sixth birthday party.

DONNACONA, QUEBEC
"Just another day," said Jean-Claude
Leveillée, with a toothpick in his mouth.
He had just returned from the former
Yugoslavia, where he'd served with the
Canadian Armed Forces as part of the
United Nations peacekeeping contingent.
"This is a crazy family," said his wife Diana,
seated behind him by the window. They
met when Jean-Claude was stationed in
Germany. She still speaks with a marked
accent. "People are much warmer in
Canada than in Germany," she said.

WITLESS BAY, NEWFOUNDLAND
Kathleen Lundrigan sits on the doorstep as her husband Louis walks down to the slipway. Inside the house, their son Thomas showed me a photograph of his grandfather. "He was a handsome man, eh?" he said. The grandfather was indeed a fine figure, formally dressed in a dark suit and tie. His hair was parted in the middle, as was the fashion in those days. As we looked at the portrait, Thomas told me a story. "The last time my father saw his father was down on the shore," he said. "That was seventy-nine years ago; Dad was only five years old. My grandfather waved to him from the boat and Dad ran along the shore as it sailed away. The schooner was headed for Barbados to purchase supplies. They never got there. They were lost at sea off the south coast about a day later. From that day on, my father had to go to work to support his family."

FLAT RIVER,
PRINCE EDWARD ISLAND
A cat named Bear rules the window ledge at Rob and Roslynn Wilby's pottery and batik studio.

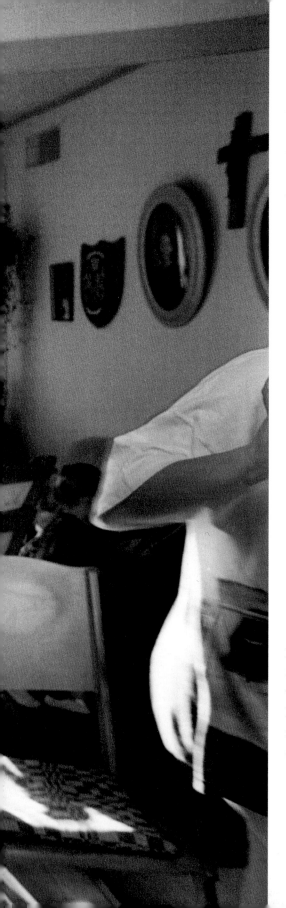

EDDIES COVE WEST, NEWFOUNDLAND
For Robert McLean, home is a place to hang his hat collection.

DONNACONA, QUEBEC
Supper's over. Dishes are washed. The party won't last long, though, because morning chores start early on a family farm.

ESKASONI, CAPE BRETON, NOVA SCOTIA

Flora Ann Joe and two other young girls had decided to spend the night camping in her family's backyard. Using a cardboard box as a makeshift drum, they sang the Micmac honour song. Overhearing this, a neighbour said it brought joy to his heart to hear the children keeping tradition alive.

STIRLING, ALBERTA

The sight of a rocking horse in the front yard made me do yet another U-turn, and I wound up staying three days at the Hogenson family farm.

At 6:30 in the morning Dave Elliot and I were riding through his calving field near Maple Creek, Saskatchewan. "Sometimes I get tired of the wind," he said. "It wears on you, day after day. Sometimes I think it's testing me." We went in for breakfast, and sat in the kitchen with his wife, Sue, after their three sons left for school. We began to talk about religion, and Dave pointed through his doorway to the open range. "My church is out there," he said.

WEST BROME, QUEBEC
Tulips wilt on the kitchen window sill in Bob Edwards' home. His wife Jean's profile is mirrored in the window as she washes the dinner dishes. In the background is the general store started by his father in 1928. Its day-to-day operation was soon to pass to the third generation, whose hopes are pinned on updating and reviving the business.

PEEL, NEW BRUNSWICK
Van Hartley, a retired auto mechanic, bought this 1950 Ford Prefect for $50, then lovingly restored it to its former glory. He and his wife lived in this house, a former stagecoach stop, for many years, before moving next door.

While I was waiting for the ferry back from Fogo Island, one of the crew displayed great interest in the camper. He asked me how many it would sleep. I told him that it could sleep his wife or girlfriend quite comfortably. "Oh, I wouldn't take them both," he replied.

IONA, CAPE BRETON, NOVA SCOTIA
Regis MacNeil takes care to dress for the occasion when she goes to collect her mail.

CAP-AUX-RETS, QUEBEC
One of Gerard Thériault's concrete sculptures, "Parler de l'est," smiles serenely over the St. Lawrence River. He designed and built his home, a cross between a teepee and a pyramid, and makes his living as a sculptor, carver, and welder, sometimes borrowing from native Canadian mythological themes.

RUSHOON, NEWFOUNDLAND
A resplendent sunrise belies the dangers of trolling for
cod from a small dory in the icy-cold Atlantic.

WORK

These days a good job is hard to find, as rural Canadians know all too well. It's a privilege to live surrounded by natural beauty, on the land or beside the ocean. But there's a price: you work longer and harder than city folks can possibly imagine. That's why it's traumatic to learn that you can't afford to be where your heart is. Some people are forced to leave, if only to make money so that they can someday return. Others choose to remain, no matter how much "better" they could do elsewhere. A regular paycheque holds no appeal; urban comforts count for little. A hired cowboy, I'm told, makes $1,000 a month for sweating or freezing on the open range. He's not in it for the money; it's in his blood. The happiest people I encountered were those who loved what they were doing, who approached their work with passion, and who were somehow connected with the romance of their daily tasks.

In some places, the work of years gone by is disappearing fast. Time-honoured lifestyles are decimated almost overnight. The forced closure of the East Coast cod fishery was taking its toll as I travelled through the Maritimes. People who for generations had earned their living from the sea suddenly found themselves with nothing to do. There isn't any counterpart to their distress. Disease may strike a cattle herd, but you restock. A farmer's land may flood or a forest may burn, but there's always next year. Not so in eastern Canada. The fishermen were limited to subsistence-level catches, enough to feed their families only. The confusion showed in their faces.

Many other communities I visited were built on natural resources, but they, too, were under increasing scrutiny. Environmental and ecological concerns had affected the fur trade and the forest and mining industries. Automation and lay-offs were the order of the day. Elsewhere the number of family farms continued to decline. From coast to coast, people wondered whether they could survive in the face of sweeping change.

Often, when I photographed people at work, I ended up giving them a hand. I dug for clams, raked Irish moss, subdued a calf, stretched a beaver, and brought in the sheaves. Without exception, everything was much more difficult than it looked.

On a fall roundup in Saskatchewan, I rode up alongside an old-timer. "You're not a city person, are you?" he said. "Nope," I replied. "I can tell that you're from the country," he said. I grew a little taller in the saddle and felt even more a part of the work at hand.

"Thank you, sir," said the cashier.

"I'm no sir, I'm a working man," said the customer.

Overheard in a general store in Newport Corner, New Brunswick

CYPRESS HILLS, SASKATCHEWAN
In the light of a foggy October dawn, cowboys ride out during the final day of the West Block cattle roundup.

PORCUPINE HILLS, ALBERTA
Flagperson Bonnie Cofield fights the October wind on Highway 2 as her co-workers inspect the newly laid surface. A rancher's wife and mother, she supplements the family income by braiding horsehair hatbands and chinstraps.

EAGLE LAKE, ONTARIO

Burton Penner follows his trapline across frozen lakes and through thick bush. "The hardest working dog on the team is the driver," he said. Home is a cabin he built from hand-felled trees and shares with his wife and their young son. He takes quiet pride in the family's self-reliance; his passion is landscape painting. Penner uses the Canadian Shield (right) as a windbreak as he boils water for soup. I travelled with Burton and his nine-dog team for three days. Late one night, while sitting around a wood stove, he recited from memory "The Cremation of Sam McGee," while stitching the shoulder seam of a new moosehide coat.

It was pitch black as we motored out of Rushoon, Newfoundland. Adrian Hunt glanced often at the radar screen. His son Paul and I sat on the engine cover behind the cabin. He told me how his brother Rick takes Dramamine every day. I bragged about all the various stunt planes and boats I'd been in and never got seasick. As we motored into the open sea, the boat began to pitch and roll. The farther out we got, the rougher it became.

For safety, Adrian decided to use the dory. He said that in "tidy seas" one had more control and reaction time with a dory than a longliner. Just as Rick and brother Wade were being dispatched in the dory, with three barrels of line with baited hooks, the sun broke the horizon and sent its rays across the rolling water to greet our bobbing boat.

Despite my seasickness, I would go again.

RUSHOON, NEWFOUNDLAND
Several miles offshore, seagulls scavenge for scraps thrown overboard as the crew clean their morning's catch of cod.

FIVE ISLANDS, NOVA SCOTIA
Women shucking clams in a canning factory react to a co-worker's off-colour observation.

MEDICINE HAT, ALBERTA
The thirty-sixth annual Spring Bull Sale at Stampede Park was a traumatic time for the Balog children (Blake, Bruce, and Rebecca), whose pet Hereford was sold at auction.

CASTLE RIVER RANGE, ALBERTA
Why did the cattle congest the road? To get to the sorting pen. This is a motorist's-eye view of the Pincher Creek Stockmens Association annual fall roundup. About twenty ranchers took part, herding new calves and yearlings down from summer pasture in the Rocky Mountain Forest Reserve.

**KENSINGTON,
PRINCE EDWARD ISLAND**
Wendy Dickieson pauses for dinner in the cab of Carl Hunter's potato harvester. The harvester looks like a metal house on wheels. It inches through the field, pulled by a tractor at a slower than walking pace. Wendy and two other women stand about ten feet off the ground, sorting spuds from stones as they roll up a conveyor belt. Watching the crews eat made me hungry. I dug up and boiled some new potatoes right there in the field, and dined on them with slices of ham.

TABER, ALBERTA
A sugar beet farmer makes sure none fall from his truck. The line of trucks waiting to weigh in at Alberta Sugar Inc. stretched for over a kilometre. After adding his delivery to the enormous pile behind him, the driver will return to his field for another load.

Willy and Alice Carpenter woke me at 9 a.m. On the tent's wood stove, Alice made a gourmet breakfast of corned beef hash, fried eggs, and potatoes, which we washed down with hot coffee.

An hour later, Willy and I were speeding out into the Beaufort Sea with Bob Grubin in Bob's boat, said to be the fastest in Tuk. With us were Bob's son Robert and Willy's son Jimmy. Our destination was Kendall Island, where the belugas feed. We spotted them from a distance and spent the next hour trying to sneak up on them.

Willy stood in the bow with his harpoon raised high. A whale rose within range. Willy threw — and just missed. We circled around for a while, but all the whales had vanished. Bob grumbled that his V-6 engine didn't just burn fuel, it drank it.

More white shapes appeared in the water. Willy got set to cast his harpoon, and Jimmy checked his rifle. Bob steered the boat while Robert navigated. Our target kept diving and surfacing. The third time it rose, Willy released the harpoon, which found its mark. The whale dove again, but resurfaced almost immediately. Jimmy aimed and fired his rifle — an amazing shot considering how the boat was pitching and tossing. The whale began to thrash about, but it was mortally wounded — shot near its blowhole, in the lungs. It made a sputtering, gurgling sound; it was drowning in its own blood. It dove again and again, each time taking longer to reappear. We thought we might have lost it, but finally it floated lifeless on the water. We towed it to shore.

The day's harvest would go into a community's shared winter food supply.

KENDALL ISLAND,
NORTHWEST TERRITORIES
Willy Carpenter of Tuktoyaktuk (opposite) aims his harpoon at a beluga whale in the Beaufort Sea. When it had been towed to shore, Jimmy Carpenter (above, with tattoo) stripped away the muktuk to reveal rich black meat, which would later be hung up to dry. Many Inuit eat the muktuk raw with a dash of bottled steak sauce or ketchup. As a guest, I was offered the very first chunk, cut from the beluga's tail.

MANOR, SASKATCHEWAN

The tool pusher, driller, derrickman, motorman, and roughnecks ready their rig for transport to another site. The oilmen work against the clock. The spring thaw is about to set in; each day's sun increases the prospect of their becoming bogged down in mud. Prairie farm boys make up most of the crew. One young roughneck said, "I'm only doing this to earn the money to buy land."

ROUYN-NORANDA, QUEBEC

Shift boss Réal Villeneuve stands outside an entrance to the Silidor gold mine. A few minutes earlier, 400 metres below ground, the temperature had been 10 degrees Celsius. Here on the surface, it's minus 40. I rode on the fender of Réal's diesel tractor through a maze of underground tunnels. The rock faces were covered with surreal streaks of bright red, blue, and yellow paint, which he explained are the geologists' universal drilling and blasting language. As we bounced stiffly along, I imagined that I was somewhere deep within an alien planet light years away.

TWIN BUTTE, ALBERTA
Blaine Marr rolls a metal feeder
across snow-covered pastureland.
Slipped over a hay bale, it will
provide a moveable feast for his
hungry yearlings.

"Look after the grass, and the grass will look after you."
A comment on overgrazing by a conservation-minded rancher in Alberta

STE-ANNE-DES-MONTS, QUEBEC
Rejean Goupil waits as his boots
are given a new lease on life by Jean
Yves Lévesque. Jean Yves insisted
on speaking English to me; he felt it
did him good to practise. He said
that when he opened the shop he
didn't know the first thing about
shoe repair. But he liked the town,
and so he dove in, learning as he
went along. His wife, Jean, is in
business also; she runs a tanning
salon in their adjacent home.

CYPRESS HILLS, SASKATCHEWAN
Once his ancestors roamed the prairies by the countless millions. Now the bison are making a comeback, both in protected areas and on ranches, where they're raised commercially for their meat and hides.

NEAR PIAPOT, SASKATCHEWAN
"Don't take my picture," the cowboy said, smiling. "If the good Lord had wanted me to be photographed, He'd have put a frame around my head."

"This job gets you into shape, then takes it out of you," says Jim Jones, who fells trees for MacMillan Bloedel. Here, he gets ready to scramble to safety, out of the way of a three-hundred-year-old Sitka spruce. Jones explained that if it fell incorrectly and broke on impact, thousands of dollars' worth of board feet would be lost. Prices vary from year to year, but a single tree can yield $30,000 in finished lumber. Jones cuts fifteen trees during an average shift. He is one of many Haida who work in the forest industry of Haida Gwaii. In the words of a co-worker, "If our trees are going to be cut down, we should be the ones that do it."

OLD MASSETT, QUEEN CHARLOTTE ISLANDS, BRITISH COLUMBIA

Jessie Hamilton prepares yellow cedar bark in her backyard. She'd spent all morning peeling it from trees in the nearby forest. Soon it will be sliced, cleaned, and tied up in neat bundles. Throughout the winter, she weaves it into traditional Haida pieces, including baskets, skirts, and hats like the one she's wearing.

FLIN FLON, MANITOBA
When the shift ends for these workers at the Hudson Bay Mining & Smelting Company, home is close by, in the shadow of the giant smokestack. The town — named after Professor Flintabbatey Flonatin, a character in J. E. P. Murdoch's novel *The Sunless City* — is built on solid rock, immediately above large deposits of gold, zinc, and copper.

LA MALBAIE, QUEBEC
Patrick Harvey rolls a log to the family sawmill, where it will be cut into slats to make shipping crates. Always smiling, he paused occasionally in his labour to caress a rosary around his neck. He attends mass twice daily, often walking the six miles to church even in the depths of winter.

STIRLING, ALBERTA
Hutterite women from the Wolf Creek colony return home after a day spent painting walls. The colony is about to expand; a draw will determine who remains at Wolf Creek and who moves to the new location.

HAWKESVILLE, ONTARIO
An Old Order Mennonite, Christian Bauman, plays fetch with his dog, Rex, using chunks of freshly plowed earth.

YATTON, ONTARIO
Old Order Mennonite teenagers pitch sheaves of wheat onto a horse-drawn wagon. I volunteered to help for a couple of hours and found it wasn't easy to stack the sheaves head-first with any degree of consistency.

It took me awhile, but I finally met up with Gary and Judy Boissineau, who run a far-flung trapline in the Algoma region. The plowed road out of Sault Ste. Marie ends in Searchmont, which consists of a gas station and a coffee shop. But Gary and Judy live about three hours beyond this point, which meant a white-knuckle drive over logging roads.

After a near-collision with another vehicle, I arrived at the place where Gary leaves his truck. He and Judy travel from there by snowmobile. They weren't expecting me, and it was too dark to follow the snowmobile tracks, so I returned to the nearest lumber camp for the night. Next day, I tried again, but still no luck. After two hours of fruitless searching on foot, I scrawled a message in the snow along the trail and retreated once again.

On my third attempt, I hitched a snowmobile ride with Jack Hotson, a conservation officer. We ran into Gary about halfway to his cabin on Trapper Lake. He'd found my note. My reward was a meal of moosemeat chili, washed down with a half-frozen bottle of wine I'd packed along. Then, he and Judy graciously insisted that I sleep in the upper bunk.

Gary told me of his concern for the animals who live in the bush. "One time, I was camping out with a friend of mine, who saw a snake sunning itself on a rock. He wanted to kill it, and I got really upset. That snake probably came every day to its favourite place, and we were just going to spend the night. I think many people concentrate on what's best for them; they act on a selfish, purely personal basis. But if you do that, you're no longer part of the system."

AUBINADONG RIVER, ONTARIO
Gary Boissineau wades through snow as he checks his trapline. "It's the moose that taught the wolf to chase," he said. "And it's the wolf that taught the moose to run."

"Those damn cows will make you grow old before your time. It's a hell of a way to live your life. You spend your summer putting twine around grass and you spend your winter taking it off."

Bill Ireland, Arcola, Saskatchewan

NEAR PIAPOT, SASKATCHEWAN
Andy Mikula instructs his grass cattle, which were eyeing greener pastures during a trail drive, to get back on track. He and twelve other riders were moving 430 head from a winter feedlot in Maple Creek to his ranch, 35 kilometres distant.

Curtis Gray, his shirt stained with blood, collected the "prairie oysters," or calves' testicles, during branding day at Rey Creek Ranch. A cowpoke named Ernie Dobson did the actual cutting. Later, the oysters were fried over an open fire. Ernie sampled one, and exclaimed, "If I'd known we'd be having these, I wouldn't have had sandwiches for lunch."

ASHCROFT, BRITISH COLUMBIA
Kurt Brown wrestles a bawling calf during branding day at the Ashcroft Ranch. In less than a minute, the animals are also vaccinated, dehorned, and castrated.

**SKINNERS POND,
PRINCE EDWARD ISLAND**

At dawn, John Ellsworth has already been out for two hours, raking the beach for Irish moss washed up by the high tide. One of its ingredients will be extracted for use in commercial food processing, but his labours are poorly rewarded: the dried moss brings only 31 cents a pound.

DONNACONA, QUEBEC

While driving down the road, I'd seen a slaughtered pig hanging in a barn doorway. I pulled into the laneway and in less-than-fluent French asked if anyone spoke English. Jean-Claude Levillée said he did, *une petite*, and that I was welcome to photograph his family. Later, I was invited to share a meal.

**DEADMAN'S BAY,
NEWFOUNDLAND**
Lobster boats are pulled up the
slipway to wait out an
approaching Atlantic storm.
Meanwhile, across the bay in
Wesleyville, a search-and-rescue
operation was being mounted for
three missing fishermen.

**PARK CORNER,
PRINCE EDWARD ISLAND**
With her sons Jason and Jeffery,
Elda Campbell waits to pick up her
husband Bruce, who has been
combining wheat all day.

With its sweet smell of burning coal and sound of metal striking metal, Vernon Walters' marine blacksmith shop is a holdover from the past. Even its thick coating of black grime dates to the nineteenth century. He still uses the original tools, hand-forged by his father and his father's father.

As he banged molten metal into the shape of hooks, the fiery glow of the forge showed the determination in his face. Like most pros, he makes what he does look easy. He spotted me as a pro, too. He gets photographed a lot by all the tourists who come to historic Lunenberg to see the *Bluenose II*. But he's a reluctant tour guide; he has work to do. Two days from now, a big order for a foreign dragger is due.

Vernon's conversation was interspersed with blows of the hammer. He'd been working all his life, he said, but he knew no other work than blacksmithing. He'd recently separated from his wife after thirty-eight years together. I asked him whether he felt responsible for the break-up. He said, "When you're married, you're always to blame."

LUNENBERG, NOVA SCOTIA
As a small boy, Vernon Walters sat on the doorstep and watched his father and grandfather as they tamed molten metal at the forge. "While other kids were playing Cowboys and Indians, I was making steel toy anchors," he said.

BONAVISTA, NEWFOUNDLAND
The idea of Away held no terrors for these three friends. Sylvia
Baker wanted to be a fashion model; Heidi Clench, a United
Church minister; and Miranda Bradley, a journalist.

COMMUNITY

Many people who live in urban centres see rural Canada as locked in place or frozen in time. Nothing could be further from the truth. Everywhere the road meets Main Street, I found communities that were far more rich and varied than they appear to the casual observer — it's just a matter of scale.

Some, of course, are a trifle more set in their ways than others. A man on Prince Edward Island told me that if a local newspaper ran an obituary of someone who came to Canada as a bride during World War II, the headline would read: "English Woman Dies in Charlottetown." But if someone was born in PEI and left as an infant for Florida, never to return, he'd be commemorated: "Island Man Dies in Sunshine State."

In rural communities there's a lot of waiting for things to happen. A barber sits in his barber's chair waiting for customers. A waitress slumps at an empty lunch counter below the Canadian flag and a picture of Elvis. Four old men and a spotted dog stand where the road bends. Vibrant young people impatiently await the day they can go take on the world. And loungers, of course, hang around, waiting for more of nothing.

On the other hand, I love the creative ways people in small corners make their own fun. Mommies kissed Santa Claus as he made his rounds. Farmers pitted their antique tractors against each other to see who could plow the straightest furrow. Trappers held contests to choose the best butts (male and female), the hairiest chest, the most impressive beer belly.

Rural Canadians claim their own and look after their own. I remember a community dinner that could have sprung from my own childhood, when Grandma DeKay and all my aunts would make a meal for all comers, presiding over a room filled with love and security, warmth, and belonging.

Sometimes outsiders, those from Away, are viewed with shyness or suspicion. But I was welcomed in the vast majority of places. If not, I simply moved on.

Most times, though, I was treated like a long-lost relative. People passed on sage advice. A barber in rural Saskatchewan remarked that since half his customers were going deaf, they didn't know what they'd heard in the first place, so were bound to muddle its retelling. "Don't believe but half the lies you hear," he said.

"Trouble is today people confuse needs and wants. They compare what they have to their neighbours; they want things they don't need. Life is a lot simpler if you just look after your needs."

Francis Power, Brigus South, Newfoundland

PORT REXTON, NEWFOUNDLAND
Neighbourhood kids play follow-the-leader along the foundation walls of a long-since dismantled barn. Watching them reminded me of my own childhood. Their games were home-made; imagination and invention ruled. Later, I found them burying each other in the tall grass. They formed human pyramids and created crazy wigs; they didn't need store-bought toys to have fun.

MITCHELL BAY, NOVA SCOTIA
Tyler Fleet tests his father's patience during Sunday worship at Saint Paul's Anglican Church.

SOURIS,
PRINCE EDWARD ISLAND
Amanda Morrow exchanges knowing whispers with Christa Cheverie while Lucas Robertson strives to maintain his cool. Local teens like to hang out outside St. Mary's Hall. Those lucky enough to have cars go peeling off in a blaze of burning rubber.

CARROLL, MANITOBA
Horses seek shelter from the blowing snow and bitter west winds.

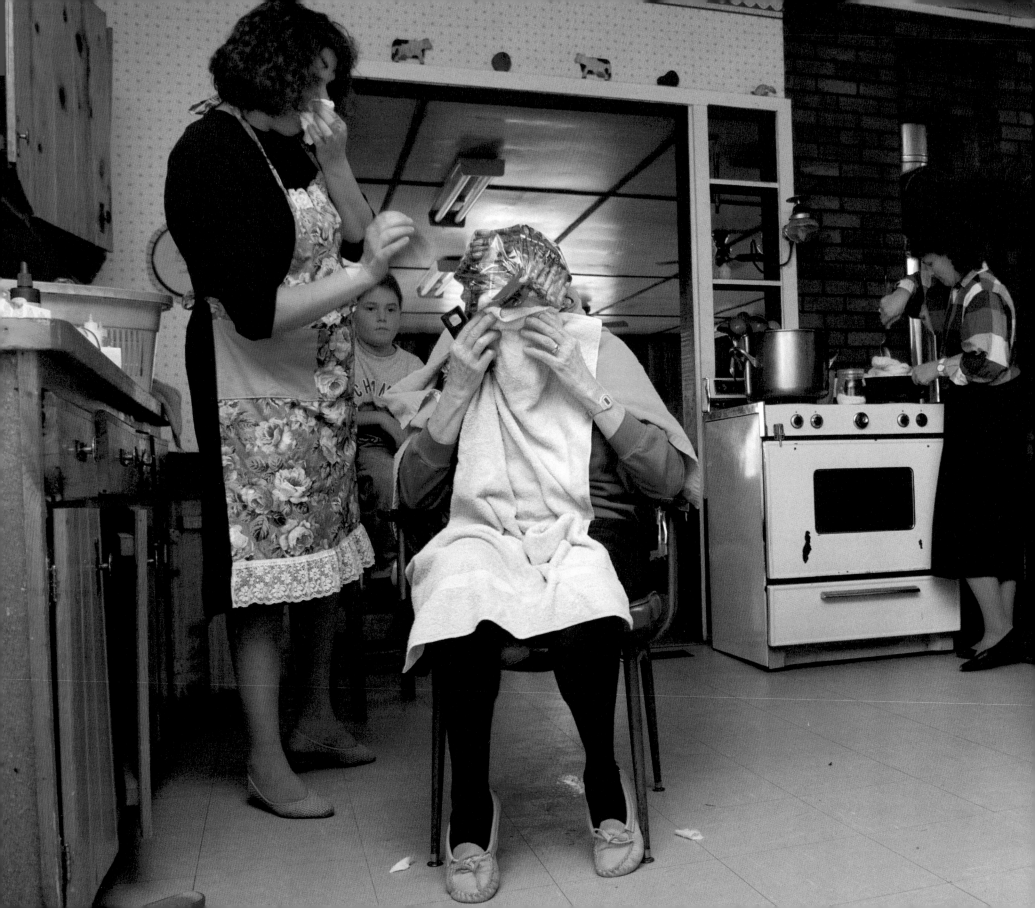

UPSALA, ONTARIO
While the noonday meal is prepared, Eloise Beebie is given an old-fashioned, don't-breath-the-fumes perm by fellow members of the Upsala Bible Centre. Later her son Eric told me, "We pass the winter on faith and run on spirit in the summer."

Tired and hungry after several hours of white-out conditions, I drove into La Ronge, Saskatchewan. My mood was as bleak as the weather. Uncertain where to park for the night, I stopped at the RCMP office. The young constable said that all the campgrounds were closed. I asked if I could park on his lot; I couldn't think of anywhere more secure. He refused, then demanded to see my identification. After taking an in-depth look at my wallet, he asked if I was someone famous. I told him I was working on it. He then said, "Are you wired?" — that is, taping him without his knowledge. I said that I was on the road, doing a book, and that all I wanted to do was to keep warm for the night. He in turn suggested that I try a hotel.

At a nearby inn, the receptionist told me I was welcome to a corner of the parking lot. Later, the same RCMP constable cruised by. He went to the check-in desk, peered out through the window, and seemed to be making a note of my licence plate.

The next morning I went inside and ordered breakfast. I was talking to the waitress, who'd just been named the province's top female bodybuilder, when the hotel manager summoned me to his office. After a lengthy calculation, he wanted to charge me $50 for parking overnight and plugging in my block heater during the meal. Since I was going to write a book, he said, I could afford to pay. In the end, he settled for $3 in loose change.

From a distance, the familiar flashes of red emergency lights caught my eye. It looked like big doings in Plaster Rock, New Brunswick — some kind of accident perhaps. Driving closer, I saw firemen. I saw where they were aiming the hoses: at the curb. This was spring cleaning. With each fire truck tankful of water, they could clean winter sand and salt from about 45 metres of curb. I watched them go through three tanks.

STANBRIDGE EAST, QUEBEC
The owner's dog, Sam, keeps watch over a sidewalk display at the Blinn's General Store.

**INUVIK,
NORTHWEST TERRITORIES**
Two friends take advantage of a level surface at the Canada Post office, their energies drained after spending six weeks canoeing on the Mackenzie River. Meanwhile, their families had shipped along a fascinating assortment of mail: cookies, chocolate bars, clean underwear, cosmetics, and the news from home.

I spent most of the day in a Canadian Tire Service bay in Stephenville, Newfoundland. I thought I only needed an oil change, but a diagnostic test indicated the battery charger was malfunctioning. It turned out to be just a scare. The truck drew a crowd of men. I heard them saying, "She's some good rig, bye" or just "She's some good, son." This, I have learned, is a high compliment.

THUNDER BAY, ONTARIO
About fifty intrepid souls took part in the Big Shiver during February's Northern Lights Winter Carnival. This involved jumping into the McIntyre River, whose waters registered 2 degrees Celsius. Once was enough for the girls at left, but some people did it twice. Having survived their dip, two men take refuge in a waiting hot tub.

BRANCH, NEWFOUNDLAND
Eric Power admonishes the neighbours' kids: "You byes stop jumping in the hay!" But to no avail. Timmy Nash makes a final dive into the sweet-smelling truckload.

ST. PETERS,
PRINCE EDWARD ISLAND
Wheat ripens around a boarded up summer home.

PORT CLEMENTS,
QUEEN CHARLOTTE ISLANDS,
BRITISH COLUMBIA
A day of truck races had conveniently produced a giant mudhole, and this daring trio couldn't resist a dip in the oozing, cooling mire.

NEAR OLD QUEBEC CITY, QUEBEC
I'd parked my camper and was settling in for the night when I saw a group of teenagers, many in costume, heading for the Halloween dance at a nearby high school.

INUVIK,
NORTHWEST TERRITORIES
It's Children's Day at the Great
Northern Arts Festival, and this
whitefish is about to be pressed into
service to decorate a T-shirt. The keys
to a good design are the moisture of
the fish, the thickness of the paint,
and the pressure used as you apply it
to the fabric. All this is ecologically
responsible as well; the fish is washed
off and used over and over again.

MASSET,
QUEEN CHARLOTTE ISLANDS,
BRITISH COLUMBIA
Rodney White is a member of the
DeChinnee dance troupe that
performed during the town's Canada
Day celebrations. He agreed to pose
with a chief's ceremonial canoe
paddle, but grew more self-conscious
and impatient with every exposure.

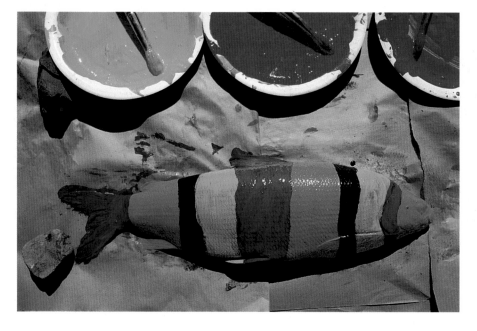

PORT CLEMENTS,
QUEEN CHARLOTTE ISLANDS,
BRITISH COLUMBIA
Pamela and Jamie Richardson flash
super-patriotic grins during Canada Day
festivities at the community park.

The town's only limousine, a blue Cadillac, was at Cindy Menchenton's house. She and six fellow graduates were posing in the backyard while their parents took snapshots. Then everyone piled into the car and took a roundabout route to Stephenville Integrated High School.

Forty-two students were graduating, and most of them had been in school together since kindergarten. A group photo taken thirteen years ago was mounted on the cafeteria wall. You could pick them out one by one; some hadn't changed very much.

After the speeches, the students removed their caps and gowns for the grand march. Families, friends, and teachers ringed the gym as the graduates paraded past in a stately fashion. When the march ended, everyone gathered in a circle beneath a cluster of balloons hanging in a net from the ceiling. The balloons floated down on cue, and the kids began to hug one another.

The prom went on until seven in the morning. There were games, a blur of virtually non-stop dancing, lots to eat, and no evidence of liquor. The grads danced with their dates and with their parents. A woman waltzed by with her son. She had tears in her eyes.

PLASTER ROCK,
NEW BRUNSWICK
Sweethearts linger behind Tobique Valley Regional High School. After thirty minutes, at the blast of an impatient car horn, the girl abruptly jumped up and sprinted off. Her mother was waiting.

STEPHENVILLE, NEWFOUNDLAND
Valedictorian Ayesha Abdeen receives the good wishes of a fellow student before graduation ceremonies.

PINCHER CREEK, ALBERTA
Rachel, a grade one student in the one-room Waterton Hutterite colony school, looks up from her math lesson. The children have two instructors: a colony member who teaches them in the German dialect their parents speak at home, and an English-speaking non-Hutterite, certified by the province. At age six, Rachel is just beginning to learn English. Later, watching the kids outside at recess, the German-speaking teacher told me that children should not develop a "playful spirit." This, he said, is "the devil's work," and distracts them from necessary tasks.

YATTON, ONTARIO
While the grown-ups are busy bringing in the sheaves, Old Order Mennonite boys frolic in a nearby field.

VULCAN, ALBERTA
These wooden skyscrapers are being displaced by elevators made of reinforced concrete — more efficient, no doubt, but far less pleasing to the eye.

SPENCES BRIDGE, BRITISH COLUMBIA
A Canadian Pacific steel gang watches the competition on the Canadian National tracks across the Fraser River.

Members of the Tsimshian
Dancers of Lax Kw'Alaams
(Port Simpson) await their cue
at the opening ceremonies of
the annual Seafest festival.

MIAMI, MANITOBA
James Waddell surveys his position
after releasing a rock. He was curling
with the Evangelical Mennonite
Church's youth team.

The first game of a brief Newfoundland summer. The day was bitterly cold, with a strong wind blowing in off the Strait of Belle Isle. I was numbed to the bone, but the kids said it was warm. Like many people in this far northern peninsula, their complexions were a soft, dusty red, like a permanent blush.

The batter is Norman Parrill, aged nineteen. I asked him whether he'd be able to find work in Eddies Cove if the fishing moratorium remained in effect. "All my friends and family are here," he said. "I wouldn't want to move away. But there's no fish."

EDDIES COVE, NEWFOUNDLAND
I wonder if a baseball game has ever been called on account of icebergs.

TWIN BUTTE, ALBERTA
While their parents attend the Shoderee Ranch's Red Angus bull sale, kids play baseball on the sort of field that dreams are made of.

**TELEGRAPH CREEK,
BRITISH COLUMBIA**
Young girls play with a sockeye salmon, netted at Six-Mile Camp along the Stikine River.

POINTE AU BARIL, ONTARIO
Andrew Dampeir looks like I felt. His hardier friend, Mark Madigan, gets an assist from his sister Heidi.

BRANCH, NEWFOUNDLAND
This evening, Patrick Power declared that he was Batman. He and his brother James, who had to settle for being Robin, wrapped white T-shirts around their heads (presumably part of a caped-crusader disguise) and grabbed a couple of sticks for swords, or maybe magic wands. The rest of the kids were having none of this, and began to pummel the superheroes in the middle of the road.

MARYSTOWN, NEWFOUNDLAND
Vanessa Strilec and Kim Snelgrove, two strippers at Wilf's Bar, use every means at their disposal to distract a pool player whom they'd challenged to a game of eight-ball. Earlier, they were sitting on the bar stools, talking. The setting sun cast a warm glow on their hair. I pointed this out, and Kim said, "You sure do know how to make a girl feel good."

RUSHOON, NEWFOUNDLAND
After the day's catch has been weighed and packed in ice, the wharf becomes a popular gathering place for young adults with nowhere else to go. The girl at right is standing on a shipping container.

**SOURIS,
PRINCE EDWARD ISLAND**
Raw recruits for the Royal Canadian Air Cadets make a first stab at basic drill techniques in the legion hall. Next week, girls will be expected to have hair pinned up off the collar, and boys, a regulation military-style buzzcut.

LA RONGE, SASKATCHEWAN
Veronica Sanderson, a Cree elder, waits in Robertson's Trading Post for a taxi to take her home after picking up her monthly pension cheque.

GARNISH, NEWFOUNDLAND
Two women photograph their neighbours after a jig's dinner at the Salvation Army hall. These dinners are very popular occasions; almost two hundred people attended.

EATONIA, SASKATCHEWAN
Mashed turnips slide into the serving bowl amidst the chaos of last-minute preparations for the Fowl Supper, a community event dating back several decades.

**FLAT RIVER,
PRINCE EDWARD ISLAND**
The Flat River Maiden strikes a pose
in front of the home and studio of
sculptor Rob Wilby. Crafted in
sculptural cement reinforced by
steel, "she is the perfect woman,"
said a grinning Rob.

DAWSON CITY, YUKON
Klondike Fever heats up the dance floor
at the sixteenth annual Dawson City
Music Festival, which attracts
entertainers and artists from across
Canada and the United States.
Cheechakos, or newcomers, come to cut
fast and loose from all over the world.

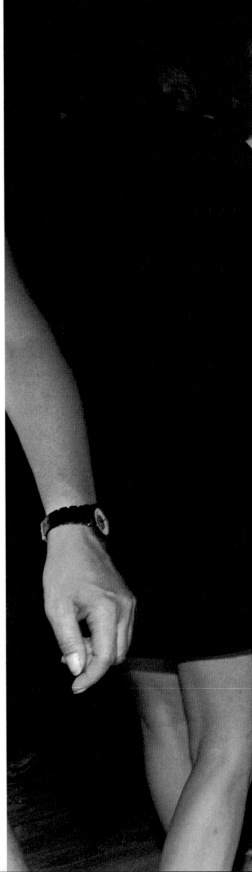

PARADISE, NOVA SCOTIA
Frank Corning challenges the neighbourhood kids to a friendly game of water pistol hide-and-seek. I asked him whether he was playing fair, given his obviously more powerful gun, and he replied, "It's them against me."

At six o'clock in the morning, I'd set up my tripod facing the Skeena Mountains at the side of the Cassiar Highway in British Columbia. A passing camper stopped, and the window was rolled down. "Are you taking a picture, or do you see something?" the tourist asked. "I'm just taking a picture," I said.

BLUE COVE, NEWFOUNDLAND
The sun dips below the Atlantic horizon and neighbours have another game of "21."

Whenever I leave a place like the Queen Charlottes — a place that I have gone out of my way to get to — I get this nagging, tugging feeling. It is often difficult to get in the truck and just drive away. I wonder: What photographs will I miss if I leave? What will I miss if I stay? In these remote places, there's no kidding myself that I can return later.

WHITEHORSE, YUKON
Two boaters head upstream past Moccasin Flats, a more or less permanent community that survives despite the efforts of city council, which has for years been threatening to annex the land. I visited John Hutch, one of the squatters, in his home. A notice on the wall proclaimed: "I Do Precision Guesswork Based on Vague Assumptions and Unreliable Data of Dubious Accuracy Provided by Persons of Questionable Intellectual Capacity."

AYR, ONTARIO
Visitors to the International Plowing Match ride back to their cars aboard a pair of hay wagons. The annual four-day event is spread out over thousands of acres of farm land, and regularly draws well over one hundred thousand people.

ST. JOHN'S, NEWFOUNDLAND
Monique Tobin, seven months pregnant with her first child, wants to
have the baby delivered at home by a local midwife.

PASSAGES

I was only passing through, but my path very often intersected with people who were, in those moments, experiencing passages of their own. I felt honoured to be a witness — and surprised to realize how many of life's major turning points can be summed up in a few simple and heartfelt, sometimes heart-rending, words: I do. You may kiss the bride. It's a girl! It's twins! We won! Good luck. You're fired. Congratulations. Nice shot, son. I'm proud of you. Bon voyage! Same time next year. Peace be with you. All my relations. Amen.

Sometimes, a simple "hello" or "goodbye" signals the most profound changes of all. I worked hard to plan my journey, for months in advance. But when it was time to leave the ones I love, morning came much too early. On the first of many nights I was to sleep alone on unfamiliar ground, I felt homesick and, at the same time, expectant about what tomorrow would bring. Each new day held the prospect of new people, new experiences, new challenges. So often, I didn't know where I was going — only that I wanted, perhaps needed, to get there. So I'd leave the known for the unknown, hesitant to press on, but certain that I had to.

In the end, I learned that the most difficult farewell of all was to the road itself. But even if you stop travelling, the journey doesn't have to end. It's an attitude, an approach to living, no matter where you may be. I came to understand this, in part, from glimpsing how others respond to the changes in the seasons, in their lives, and in the places they call home.

Along the way, to mark an important passage in my life, it was only fitting that I acquired a new name. My Micmac friends supplied it. It seems that William DeKay translated as Sullian Suglugat. Translated back into English, that's Billy Rotten. It's not in the same league as Dances with Wolves, but it will have to do.

RANKIN INLET,
NORTHWEST TERRITORIES
Elsie Evyagotailak swings from the
arms of her parents Susie and Joe.
Susie made every stitch of their
clothing by hand, including the
mukluks. The family had flown in
from Coppermine, in the western
Arctic, to attend ceremonies
honouring Queen Elizabeth, who
was keeping a promise to visit
someday. An attempt to do so
during a previous royal tour had
been grounded by bad weather. I
came by air, too, from Inuvik. The
Queen and I faced the same
predicament; no roads lead to this
remote Hudson Bay community.

WESLEYVILLE, NEWFOUNDLAND
Edwin Mayo proudly takes his first
child for a stroll. Janessa, seven
weeks old, is the centre of attention,
and with good reason. "We were
told that we couldn't have any
children," he said. "But after fifteen
years my wife Judy came down with
a virus, and here we are."

Yvonno Kaput was buried today. His family said that they'd be honoured if I attended the funeral and made photographs; they gave me a ride to the cemetery in their pickup truck. I stayed behind the mourners, trying to be unobtrusive. I got the sense that I was welcome.

After the burial I returned to the home of a grade six schoolteacher, a white man, with whom I was staying. My glasses were wet with rain and beginning to fog up — I could barely see as I stepped inside. He asked me how many pictures I'd taken, and I replied, "About ten."

Suddenly he struck me with his fist. My glasses flew off, and he hit me a second time. I saw stars. He pushed me through the door, out into the rain. I could have my luggage, he shouted from the door, but only if I gave him the roll of film. He felt that I had disgraced his home. He had to live there, but I was passing through.

Argument was useless; the luggage contained all my film and photo gear. What else could I do? I handed over the roll.

When Yvonno Kaput's father heard about the incident, he said: "This man has dishonoured our family." The young widow and her sister-in-law retrieved my film from the schoolteacher and returned it to me the next day.

RANKIN INLET, NORTHWEST TERRITORIES
Relatives and friends grieve for Yvonno Kaput, who died along with two others in a boating accident on Hudson Bay.

BURDETT, ALBERTA

Les McIntyre, the auctioneer, takes bids on a tractor belonging to Roy and Tina Vos. Most of the people in attendance were their immediate neighbours, but some had come from as far away as the southwestern states.

Roy and Tina were leaving their 810-hectare farm for good and selling everything except a few personal possessions. They planned to travel the country in a motor home; they hoped to see every province, and much of the United States.

"You know," he said, "the hardest thing to part with today was the tractor. Spring, summer, fall, all I did was drive tractor. I sold the farm to three young fellows under forty. I had a good life off of it, but the bigger the farm, the harder they fall. As of now, we're fully retired."

STIRLING, ALBERTA

A lone gull stretches its wings above a storage bin at the Wolf Creek Hutterite colony.

The group known as the Inspirada Americana is based in Alaska, but travels throughout the North. One of its purposes is to help aboriginal peoples maintain or reclaim their oral traditions, which have been lost or fragmented over time.

This year's annual Moosehide Gathering was very special. Moosehide is the site of a Tr'ondek Hwech'in village in Yukon Territory whose peaceful existence was shattered by the Yukon Gold Rush in the 1890s. The Han First Nation realized that their culture was at grave risk. Chief Isaac, their farsighted leader, travelled to Tanacross, Alaska, and entrusted to its residents his village's most sacred lore, in the form of songs. He also left with them a symbolic dancing stick known as a gun hawk, but asked that it be returned one day.

Thanks to Chief Isaac, the Han's traditions were kept alive through many generations. Today, the gun hawk was restored to its owners, as the story of Moosehide and its people was sung for the first time in over a hundred years.

This was cause for celebration, and the gathering was well attended, partly because it kicked off the day after the Dawson Music Festival ended. Dawson is about fifteen minutes downstream by boat, and many whites had come to get into the spirit of the event. Some wore tie-dyed clothing and had braided their hair. Germans, who are amazingly enthusiastic about aboriginal cultures, were well represented. Actually, the whole affair was a miniature United Nations. I met Ehab (Abe) Ibrahim, a Sudanese Muslim who was travelling around the North, looking for work as a bush pilot. He wanted to go to Inuvik, but his car was unsuited to the rigours of the Dempster Highway, so he caught a ride with me. This is not a road to be taken lightly. In summer, its surface is covered with choking dust, known as Dempster Flour; a tankful of gas along the way cost $60. Upon arrival, Abe discovered a number of Sudanese families living in Inuvik, where they specialize in driving cab.

MOOSEHIDE, YUKON
Fifteen-year-old Leslie Jackson escorts elders Annie Henry and Mary Bittrewka to a salmon supper feast. Elders are the first to eat, as a mark of respect. Later, Inspirada Americana invited everyone to join in the dance.

SYDNEY RIVER, CAPE BRETON, NOVA SCOTIA

Darren and Keith Chomyn join their father Don atop their vacation home. They'd headed east from Alberta and had been on the road for three months. I asked if the amazing pile of goods strapped to the car had attracted the attention of the police. Don said that as long as the "stuff" was secured, it posed no problem. He'd had lots of double-takes, but no tickets. He went on to explain that his wife had died of cancer a short while back. "The boys really miss their mother," he said. "We're still hurting badly."

QUEEN CHARLOTTE CITY, BRITISH COLUMBIA

Annick Blais and Francis Madore, two young Quebeckers, were taking a week's vacation from their summer job, planting trees for a forestry firm. I was glad to have company, and agreed to drive them to Masset, where they planned to camp on the beach.

MEDICINE HAT, ALBERTA
The approach to fences varies across
Canada. Some are made of rocks,
some of wood, some of wire. Design
and construction vary, but what
remains is a down-home respect for
neighbours' fences — a value that has
weathered the test of time.

KISPIOX, BRITISH COLUMBIA
After the Cowboy Prayer is read, a
saddle bronc rider braces himself
for eight seconds of hard travelling
at the Kispiox Valley Rodeo.

WITLESS BAY, NEWFOUNDLAND
Louis Lundrigan, on his evening walk
to the slipway. He often pauses to
rest, leaning against one of the many
fishing boats that lie disused and
decaying. "It's a graveyard, it really
is," said his son Thomas.

"Old men get the glory, but old women live longer."
Retired school teacher Maxine Parker, Stickney, New Brunswick

AYLESBURY, SASKATCHEWAN
As a girl, Myrna Luther came north
from Minnesota with her parents.
She married an Aylesbury man,
Martin Luther, and together they
bought some land and raised a
family. Her husband is dead now;
her children grown and gone.
Myrna named the place herself. She
told me it seemed like an obvious
description in those days.

**PARK CORNER,
PRINCE EDWARD ISLAND**
Seeing Jeffery Campbell and his father Bruce reminded me of my own childhood. I spent many hours riding shotgun in a combine, learning to love the land and counting the days until I could slide over and help steer.

GLENAVON, SASKATCHEWAN
Wilf Stamm had spent the entire day repainting this 1936 McCormick threshing machine. His son had chided him about lavishing attention on a piece of equipment that hadn't seen active service for many a year, so Wilf felt vindicated by the fact that a total stranger wanted to photograph his handiwork. "I'd rather wear out than rust out," he said.

AFTON, NOVA SCOTIA
Mary Rose Gould devotes herself
to crafting traditional Micmac
wooden baskets. She displayed and
sold a selection of them at the
weekend powwow.

YELLOWKNIFE,
NORTHWEST TERRITORIES
Just your typical media scrum. The
chief had taken part in ceremonies
held in honour of Queen Elizabeth
and Prince Philip, who were
inspecting native cultural displays in
Fred Henne Territorial Park.

Affection says 'tis hard to part,
Nor can we well from tears refrain.
But this reflection cheers the heart,
We only part to meet again.

A plaque erected in St. Paul's Church, Trinity, Newfoundland,
to the memory of Thomas Verge, who died, aged twenty, in 1840

CYPRESS HILLS, SASKATCHEWAN
Sun-bleached elk antlers adorn a weathered tool shed beneath the endless prairie sky.

STANBRIDGE EAST, QUEBEC
Ceddy Lawlor sits cheerfully on his tombstone in the Hillside Harris Cemetery. This is not a misprint. Back in 1989, after several days of non-stop drinking, Ceddy decided that he would surely die later that year. There happened to be a sale on tombstones at the time, so Ceddy bought one for himself and his brother, Halo. When I came by, Halo was alive and well. So was Ceddy, except for a touch of the gout.

LAWLOR
CEDDY LAWLOR
1934—1989
GONE BUT NOT FORGOTTEN
HALO LAWLOR
1941

Never have I been surrounded by so many floral-print dresses. Fifteen princesses were in the running for the title of Apple Blossom Queen. An important part of the competition was this afternoon's tea, when each princess had to give a two-minute speech, without benefit of notes. When a girl faltered we tried to will her into an on-the-spot recovery. Later, at the Queen's Ball, the new queen and all the princesses assembled before making their grand entrance. People hovered around the door, peeking in. One woman said to another, "She's so beautiful! Which one is she?"

OLD QUEBEC CITY, QUEBEC
The clock strikes midnight at a Halloween party in the Théâtre Capitole. Everybody was up dancing, except this exhausted clown; even my camera flash failed to rouse him from his slumber.

KENTVILLE, NOVA SCOTIA
Most Original Costume contestants make their way along Main Street during the annual Apple Blossom Festival Children's Parade.

Today was my friend Declan's memorial in Washington, D.C. I memorialized him with a sweat at White Bear Lake, Saskatchewan. Compared with my two previous sweats, this was hotter. The towel around me provided a scant shield. It took all my mental energy not to bolt for the door. In the darkness of the small space, men are united in prayer and remembrance. The leader poured more water on the glowing rocks. More steam.

My mind wandered back down the road, rewinding. How will I remember Declan Haun? It goes far beyond the picture editing and technical guidance over these last nine months on the road. I'll miss his enthusiasm and encouragement and believe they will live on. I'll miss his being there for me at all hours, listening, boosting my confidence. One couldn't ask for a better mentor or truer friend. And yes, Declan, I'm shooting more landscapes.

PHEASANT RUMP RESERVE, SASKATCHEWAN
The remains of a sweat lodge stand near Medicine Wheel Hill on Nakota First Nation land, near the community of Kisbey.

Anne-Marie Comeau, the leader of La Baie en Joie, invited me to photograph them performing a piece titled "Partons, La Mer Est Belle." It tells the story of a fisherman who's been lost at sea, and of his wife, who laments his untimely death.

I was struck by the patience and professionalism of these young women. We spent two hours on the windswept beach, at twilight. Their costumes provided scant protection against the cold, but they never hesitated or complained.

They explained that in order to convey the emotions behind the dance, they were required to act as well. They used various devices to summon up a mood of bereavement and desolation. One revealed that she pictured her grandmother, who'd recently passed away. "When I was looking at the sky, that's exactly what I was thinking of, because I couldn't visualize a boat," she said. Another imagined how she would feel if she were married and her husband were to die. "Really sad," she said. "Really, really sad." A third added that the fear of death was actual and immediate for her; both her parents fished. "It's a way of life," she said. "You do it even though you know you'll probably be hurt. You take tremendous risks, but people have to go out. Fishing is what our town is based on. Besides, a lot of people don't have the education to do anything else."

METEGHAN, NOVA SCOTIA
Members of the Acadian dance troupe La Baie en Joie huddle amidst piercing winds on the beach during low tide.

INUVIK,
NORTHWEST TERRITORIES
Newlyweds Mandy and Trevor
Kaglik leave the Christian
Assembly Church, accompanied
by Trevor's grandmother.

AFTON, CAPE BRETON, NOVA SCOTIA
Tashia Lafford hugs her father John as
they sit on a picnic table after
breakfast at the annual powwow.

STE-CHRISTINE, QUEBEC
Jean-Paul St. Amour, in plaid shirt, ushers Gilles Gauthier of St-Théodore-d'Acton through a forest he planted in the early 1950s. Both men had heard of the other's lifelong passion but had never actually met. Between them they've converted hundreds of hectares of marginal farmland into thriving evergreen forests. Gauthier was in awe of St. Amour's achievements. He turned to me and humbly indicated that St. Amour's forest was better than his.

Gilles Gauthier's family was surprised to hear him speaking with me in English. I explored the limits of my French, too, during our time together over five days.

His friend and neighbour Julie Herr helped us out whenever we needed a translator. Gilles is a very modest man, so Julie filled me in on his work.

"He started planting trees in the 1940s, on his father's farm," she said. "It was not fashionable to be conscious of the environment in those days. He did it because he wanted to. I don't know if the community recognizes his accomplishments. He feels he's an ordinary guy who does ordinary things in his ordinary town.

"I think there are many others like Gilles, but we don't hear about them. He taught me that if you take one step at a time, you can have an influence on the environment around you. I hope I have as much energy when I'm seventy-six. He invests his own money and his own time; nobody has ever paid him a cent.

"Over the years, he's probably planted a quarter-million trees. He's given gifts of a thousand trees at a time to local kids, because they're the future generation. Some grandfathers have candies in their pockets, but his are full of seeds."

WALLENSTEIN, ONTARIO
Less than two weeks after fire
destroyed Karen and Ray
Martin's barn, 350 members of
the Mennonite community
gathered to help them rebuild.
Two days later, the dairy herd was
safe in its new home.

GRAND FALLS, NEW BRUNSWICK
Contestants for the title of First
Harley Fest Queen applaud the
winner. So, off-camera, do numerous
bikers, whose enthusiasm knew no
bounds. They'd already made their
preferences known, during both the
talent and swimwear competitions.

BURMIS, ALBERTA
The Burmis Tree has marked the gateway to the Crowsnest Pass since Canadian National Railway surveyors first scouted the area in search of a route through the Rocky Mountains in the 1880s.

LONG ISLAND, NEWFOUNDLAND
Former islanders gather around a bonfire on the beach at Port Royal. Twenty-five years ago these families relocated to the mainland. At that time many small outports were depopulated, and residents were given financial incentives to move. Some people built new homes; others floated their old houses to new sites, by raft.

Today, friends met again, many for the first time in a quarter-century. The reunion committee had fashioned a dance hall with a wooden floor and thin plastic sheeting for roof and walls. The night was rainy and the roof leaked, but that didn't deter the celebrants, who partied until dawn.

RANKIN INLET,
NORTHWEST TERRITORIES
By next day, snow was falling; ice
was forming. Summer was over.

WESLEYVILLE, NEWFOUNDLAND
Family and friends comfort Chris
Goodyear and Dwayne Howell as they
leave the cemetery where Raymond
Howell has just been buried.

I spent my thirty-first birthday waiting in cold silence while fishermen dragged the bottom of Bonavista Bay, near Wesleyville, Newfoundland, for the body of Raymond Howell.

Raymond went out yesterday afternoon to check his lobster traps with his son Dwayne and his grandson Christopher Goodyear. An hour later, they capsized and were thrown overboard. They managed to reach the boat and cling to its keel. The younger men began to lose their grip, but Raymond summoned the last of his energy and supported them. Then he too began to tire. His last words were, "Now remember, byes, stay with the boat." Then he disappeared beneath the surface.

For four hours Dwayne and Christopher tried to guide the boat toward a nearby island. They were able to get very close to shore, but a treacherous undertow prevented them from swimming the final distance. When they felt the motor scrape against a rock, they swam — then crawled — the last few feet to safety. They huddled together in the open, overnight.

A number of fishing comrades spent the night at sea, but without success. The next morning Woodrow Kelloway and Cyril Best spotted the boat, still floating. At first they thought they saw two large birds perched on a rock. Then they realized that the figures were the missing men. "If we'd never found them for another hour, God knows what would have happened," said Kelloway. "They came to the boat arm in arm, like when you get married, each feller keeping the other up. All through the night, they took turns moving one another's legs. They didn't go to sleep; they were afraid they might not wake up."

Both men survived. Divers found Raymond Howell's body the next day. The following day, he was buried. He was only fifty-nine, and had planned to retire within two weeks, to spend more time with his family.

Over a snack of moose jerky and rhubarb wine, Jean Canouts said that her main ambitions in life had been to be as good a cook as her mother and to have a dog team. At one time, in fact, she used sled dogs to travel her trapline near Searchmont, Ontario, but now she has a snowmobile. She also wanted to be a vet, a goal she didn't achieve. "When other children were going to school, I was learning how to raise hell and live in the bush," she said. "But I have no regrets. If I can't do it tomorrow, I don't feel bad because I did it yesterday."

WOOD'S HARBOUR,
NOVA SCOTIA
Newlyweds Lisa and Robert Leary were chauffeured from Calvary United Baptist Church by limousine. After tying the knot, the wedding party, composed of Robert's fellow Mounties, formed an honour guard.

**SEACOW POND,
PRINCE EDWARD ISLAND**
A horse shares its grazing pasture with a longliner sitting idle onshore because of the cod-fishing moratorium.

**CAMPBELLS POND,
PRINCE EDWARD ISLAND**
Lindsay Michael and Camille Labchuk savour their fifteen minutes of fame as stand-ins during the filming of the popular television series "Road to Avonlea." The following day, it was back to school.

ST-HENRI-DE-TAILLON, QUEBEC
A statue of Jesus stimulates the morning air
outside the parish church.

ON THE ROAD

While travelling across Canada I met hundreds of people who took time out from their routines to assist me.
You know who you are and I thank you — it was teamwork all the way.

The following is a list of people and places where I stayed during my journey. In most cases I either billeted in homes or slept in my camper in driveways or parking lots.

1993

April 5 — Dan DeKay, Lindsay, Ontario (house)

April 6 — Martha Nelson, Bill Gallagher and children, Ottawa, Ontario (house)

April 7 — Chrystal King and Brad Hadfield, Ottawa, Ontario (house)

April 8 — Shirley Stikeman, Montreal, Quebec (camper)

April 9 — Bob and Jean Edwards, West Brome, Quebec (camper)

April 10 — Salle Memorial Hall, Stanbridge East, Quebec (camper)

April 11-14 — Bruce Baker, Stanbridge East, Quebec (camper)

April 15-19 — Stephane Gauthier and Louiselle Menard, St-Théodore-d'Acton, Quebec (house)

April 20-22 — Christine Fiset, Jacques Trembly and children, Charlesbourg, Quebec City, Quebec (camper)

April 23 — Denis and Denise Fournier and children, St-Michel, Quebec (camper)

April 24 — Clement Dubé, Guyonne Brazeau and children, Rivière-Ouelle, Quebec (camper)

April 25 — Jardins de Métis, Quebec near Ste-Luce — I stopped at the entrance to this park; it was closed for the season (camper)

April 26 — Françoise and Valere Turcotte, Val-Brillant, Quebec (camper)

April 27 — Richard Adams, Matapédia, Quebec (house)

April 28 — Richard Adams, Matapédia, Quebec (camper)

April 29-30 — Leopold Roy, St-Quentin, New Brunswick (camper)

May 1 — Volunteer Fire Department driveway, Grand Falls, New Brunswick (camper)

May 2 — Willard and Jeanne Higgins, Anfield, New Brunswick (camper)

May 3 — Catholic Church Mission, Arthurette, New Brunswick (camper)

May 4 — Robert and Elizabeth Nielsen, Kilburn, New Brunswick (camper)

May 5-6 — Chris and Sonja Bschaden and children, Centreville, New Brunswick (camper)

May 7-11 — Faye and Peter Vido and children, Lower Kintore, New Brunswick (camper)

May 12 — Lucille Horrelt, Nackawic, New Brunswick (camper)

May 13 — Petro-Canada station next to laundromat in Fredericton, New Brunswick (camper)

May 14 — Saint John to Digby ferry (Princess of Acadia) parking lot, Saint John, New Brunswick (camper)

May 15 — Halifax International Airport parking lot, Nova Scotia (camper)

May 16 — Hockey Arena, Chester, Nova Scotia (camper)

May 17 — Evelyn and Percy Langille, Big Tancook Island, Nova Scotia (house)

May 18-19 — Kim Smith, The Dory Shop, Lunenburg, Nova Scotia (camper)

May 20 — St. Alban's Anglican Church parking lot, Volger's Cove, Nova Scotia (camper)

May 21 — Millstone Bed and Breakfast, Shelburne, Nova Scotia

May 22 — Barrington Area Lions Community Hall parking lot, Woods Harbour, Nova Scotia (camper)

May 23 — Yarmouth ferry dock (Scotia Prince), Nova Scotia (camper)

May 24 — On a deadend road, Rockville, Nova Scotia (camper)

May 25-26 — Meteghan River, about 30 feet from the Atlantic on a stretch of beach, Nova Scotia (camper)

May 27-29 — Baseball park parking lot, Kentville, Nova Scotia (camper)

May 30 — Noel Shore Cemetery in front of church, Lower Selma, Nova Scotia (camper)

May 31-June 2 — Barbara, Joan and Audrey Lewis, Lower Five Islands, Nova Scotia (camper)

June 3 — Robbie Smith, Five Islands, Nova Scotia (camper)

June 4 — Valerie Wilson, Halifax, Nova Scotia (camper)

June 5 — Angella McIntyre-Geddes, Moser River, Nova Scotia (camper)

June 6 — Parking lot, Sherbrooke, Nova Scotia (camper)

June 7 — Elizabeth and Robert Pelley and children, Sunnyville, Nova Scotia (camper)

June 8 — Cape Breton Island tourist office parking lot just off the causeway, Nova Scotia (camper)

June 9 — Ponville Beach Picnic Area, Department of Natural Resources, Isle Madame, Nova Scotia (camper)

June 10 — Wood Avenue across the street from Patty Griffen's home (camper)

June 11-14 — Glayan and Denise Wujcik and children, Glace Bay, Cape Breton Island, Nova Scotia (camper)

June 15-18 — Dave and Helen Rex and family, Stephenville, Newfoundland (camper)

June 19 — Rocky Harbour Fun Park parking lot, Newfoundland (camper)

June 20 — Maynard's Motor-Inn paarking lot, Hawke's Bay, Newfoundland (camper)

June 21 — Blue Cove Fishing Wharf, Newfoundland (camper)

June 22 — Viking Mall parking lot, St. Anthony, Newfoundland (camper)

June 23 — In an open field about 30 feet from the Strait of Belle Isle, Eddies Cove, Newfoundland (camper)

June 24 — In a gravel quarry along the ocean between Barr'd Harbour and Eddies Cove West, Newfoundland (camper)

June 25-27 — Dave and Helen Rex and family, Stephenville, Newfoundland (camper)

June 28 — Ultramar Gas Station parking lot, Corner Brook, Newfoundland (camper)

June 29 — Chrysler-Plymouth dealership parking lot, Grand Falls, Newfoundland (camper)

June 30 — Along the Twillingate Light House road, Newfoundland (camper)

July 1 — Leo and Bonnetta Snow and family, Wings Point, Fogo District, Newfoundland (camper)

July 2 — Lewisporte Marine Centre parking lot, Newfoundland (camper)

July 3 — Cyril, Paula and Ryan McGrath, Tilting, Newfoundland (camper)

July 4 — Rosemary and Austin Hart, Fogo Island, Newfoundland (camper)

July 5 — Violet and Barry Pennell, Carmanville, Newfoundland (camper)

July 6-7 — Wesleyville Marine Centre wharf, Newfoundland (camper)

July 8 — Beside Burry's Groceteria Food Town, Greenspond, Newfoundland (camper)

July 9 — Wesleyville Marine Centre wharf, Newfoundland (camper)

July 10 — Winter Brook Development Association Office and Meeting Room parking lot, Port Bandford, Newfoundland (camper)

July 11-13 — On a dirt side road in Cape Bonavista, Newfoundland (camper)

July 14-16 — Ruth Lawrence, Chuck Herriott and Luke Lawrence, Goose Cove, Newfoundland (camper)

July 17 — Government wharf, Trinity, Newfoundland (camper)

July 18 — Irving gas/truck stop, Whitbourne, Newfoundland (camper)

July 19-23 — Pat and Marilyn Clarke, Goulds, Newfoundland (house)

July 24-31 — Flew back to Ontario — George DeKay, Hyde Park (house)

August 1 — Greg Locke and Monique Tobin, St. John's, Newfoundland (house)

August 2 — Pat and Marilyn Clarke, Goulds, Newfoundland (camper)

August 3 — Our Lady of Assumption Church parking lot, Point La Haye, Newfoundland (camper)

August 4 — Shopping mall parking lot, Placentia, Newfoundland (camper)

August 5 — Greg Locke and Monique Tobin, St. John's, Newfoundland (house)

August 6-7 — Elaine Hann and family, Port Royal, Long Island Reunion, Newfoundland (tent)

August 8 — Irving gas/truck stop, Trans-Canada and Hwy 210, Newfoundland (camper)

August 9-10 — Government wharf, Rushoon, Newfoundland (camper)

August 11 — Shopping mall parking lot, Marystown, Newfoundland (camper)

August 12 — Government wharf, Garnish, Newfoundland (camper)

August 13-16 — Greg Locke and Monique Tobin, St. John's, Newfoundland (house)

August 17 — Cape St. Mary's Ecological Reserve parking lot, Newfoundland (camper)

August 18 — Coast Guard parking lot, North Sydney, Nova Scotia (camper)

August 19 — Beside the Greenwood United Church, Cape Breton Island, Nova Scotia (camper)

August 20 — Parking lot at Cape Breton Exhibition grounds parking lot, North Sydney, Nova Scotia (camper)

August 21 — Cheticamp harbour parking lot, Cabot Trail, Cape Breton Island, Nova Scotia (camper)

August 22 — Kenny and Frances Googoo, Eskasoni Reserve, Cape Breton Island, Nova Scotia (camper)

August 23-25 — George Francis, Eskasoni Reserve, Cape Breton Island, Nova Scotia (camper)

August 26 — St. Mary's Catholic Church parking lot, Mabou, Cape Breton Island, Nova Scotia (camper)

August 27 — Coast Guard parking lot, North Sydney, Nova Scotia (camper)

August 28 — With the Men of the Deep in Pictou, Nova Scotia (fishery dorm)

August 29 — Joanne and Fred Gillis, Dominion, Nova Scotia (house)

August 30-31 — George Francis, Eskasoni Reserve, Cape Breton Island, Nova Scotia (camper)

September 1 — Irving gas/truck stop just west of Cape Breton causeway, Nova Scotia (camper)

September 2-September 6 — Flew back to Ontario — the Pistritto family, Toronto

September 7 — Northumberland Ferry Limited parking lot, Caribou, Nova Scotia (camper)

September 8 — Norman and Annie Rankin, Charlottetown, Prince Edward Island (camper)

September 9 — Robert and Roslynn Wilby, Flat River, Prince Edward Island(camper)

September 10 — George Francis, Eskasoni Reserve, Cape Breton Island, Nova Scotia (camper)

September 11-12 — Irving gas/truck stop, just west of Cape Breton causeway, Nova Scotia (camper)

September 13 — Sturgeon Waterbreak driveway, Prince Edward Island (camper)

September 14 — Souris beach parking lot, Prince Edward Island (camper)

September 15 — St. Peters Circle Club parking lot, Prince Edward Island (camper)

September 16 — Brackley Beach parking lot, Prince Edward Island National Park (camper)

September 17-19 — Robert and Roslynn Wilby, Flat River, Prince Edward Island (camper)

September 20 — On road in front of Tim Woolner's residence, Charlottetown, Prince Edward Island (camper)

September 21 — Evelyn and Wade Gallichon, Souris, Prince Edward Island (camper)

September 22 — Ruby and Horace Burgoyne, Kensington, Prince Edward Island (house)

September 23 — Royal Canadian Legion Branch No. 9 parking lot, Kensington, Prince Edward Island (camper)

September 24 — Robert and Roslynn Wilby, Flat River, Prince Edward Island(camper)

September 25 — Afton Reserve Powwow grounds, Prince Edward Island (camper)

September 26 — Northumberland Ferry Limited parking lot, Caribou, Nova Scotia (camper)

September 27-28 — Robert and Roslynn Wilby, Flat River, Prince Edward Island (camper)

September 29 — Ruby and Horace Burgoyne, Kensington, Prince Edward Island (house)

September 30-October 1 — John and Donna Lee Ellsworth and family, Skinners Pond, Prince Edward Island (camper)

October 2-6 — Barry Philp and Brenda Dereniuk, Kensington, Prince Edward Island (house)

October 7 — Richard Guertin, Charlottetown, Prince Edward Island (house)

October 8 — Tina Bourgeois, parking lot, Charlottetown, Prince Edward Island (camper)

October 9-11 — Robert and Roslynn Wilby, Flat River, Prince Edward Island (camper)

October 12 — Murray Corner First United Church parking lot, New Brunswick (camper)

October 13 — Irving gas/truck stop parking lot, south of Woodstock, New Brunswick (camper)

October 14 — Faye and Peter Vido and children, Lower Kintore, New Brunswick (camper)

October 15 — Lucy's Truck Stop Restaurant parking lot, Burnt Church, New Brunswick (camper)

October 16 — Tourist office parking lot, Tracadie, New Brunswick (camper)

October 17 — Wilma and Dan Murphy, Bathurst, New Brunswick (camper)

October 18 — Restaurant parking lot, Matapédia, Quebec (camper)

October 19 — St. Andrews United Church parking lot, New-Richmond, Quebec (camper)

October 20 — Parking lot in Percé, Quebec (camper)

October 22 — Street corner in Rivière-au-Renard, Quebec (camper)

October 23 — Parking lot in Ste-Anne-des-Monts, Quebec (camper)

October 24 — Petro-Canada service station, Matane, Quebec (camper)

October 25 — On side street in Shawinigan, Quebec (camper)

October 26-27 — Parked on 57e rue Ouest, Charlesbourg, Quebec (camper)

October 28 — De La Capitale Dodge Chrysler Ltee. parking lot, Quebec City, Quebec (camper)

October 29-31 — YMCA de Quebec parking lot, Quebec City, Quebec (camper)

November 1 — Promenades Ste-Anne Centre Designer Factory Outlet parking lot, Beaupré, Quebec (camper)

November 2-4 — IGA food store parking lot, Baie-St-Paul, Quebec (camper)

November 5 — Clermont Dodge Chrysler Inc. parking lot, Clermont, Quebec(camper)

November 6 — Ultramar parking lot in Chicoutimi, Quebec (camper)

November 7-8 — Depanneur Proprio Accommodation 8 à 11 store parking lot, Chicoutimi, Quebec (camper)

November 9 — Petro-Canada parking lot, St-Henri-de-Taillon, Quebec (camper)

November 10 — NJN Motosport Inc. parking lot, St-Prime, Quebec (camper)

November 11 — Shell service station parking lot, Desbiens, Quebec (camper)

November 12-16 — Mark Côté and Marichka, Baie-St-Paul, Quebec (house)

November 17 — Irving gas/truck station, Clermont, Quebec (camper)

November 18 — Xavier parking lot, Petite-Rivière-St-François, Quebec (camper)

November 19 — YMCA de Quebec parking lot, Quebec City, Quebec (camper)

November 20 — Ultramar gas station parking lot, Deschambault, Quebec(camper)

November 21 — Olca gas station parking lot, Cap-de-la-Madeleine, Quebec(camper)

November 22 — Petro-Canada gas station parking lot, St-Faustin, Quebec(camper)

November 23 — Restaurant Bachelors Chambres parking lot, Louvicourt, Quebec (camper)

November 24-25 — Gaston Proulx, Sullivan, Quebec (camper)

November 26-27 — Le Motel Journey's End parking lot, Val-d'Or, Quebec (camper)

November 28 — Le Motel Journey's End parking lot, Rouyn-Noranda, Quebec (camper)

November 29 — Silidor Mines parking lot, Rouyn-Noranda, Quebec (camper)

November 30 — The Bunker (Military Museum in the Ontario Northland Railway station) parking lot, Cobalt, Ontario (camper)

December 1 — Dan DeKay, Lindsay, Ontario (house)

December 2 - January 6 — Refuelled with Paula DeKay, Mike and Chris DeKay and George DeKay in Windsor, London and Hyde Park, Ontario

1994

January 7 — Holiday Inn parking lot, Barrie, Ontario (camper)

January 8 — Miracle Mart parking lot, Sudbury, Ontario (camper)

January 9-12 — Bob and Maxine Pollock, Richards Landing, Ontario (house)

January 13 — Dead Lake Jobber's Camp, Dead Lake Road, Algoma, Ontario (camper)

January 14 — Moya Morrow and John Payne, Sault Ste Marie, Ontario (house)

January 15 — Gary and Judy Boissineau, Trapper Lake, Ontario (camp cabin)

January 16-17 — Gary and Judy Boissineau, Heyden, Ontario (house)

January 18 — Jean and Vinnie Canouts, Ranger Lake Road, Searchmont, Ontario (house)

January 19-20 — Gary and Judy Boissineau, Heyden, Ontario (house)

January 21-22 — Gary and Judy Boissineau, Trapper Lake, Ontario (camp cabin)

January 23-24 — Gary and Judy Boissineau, Heyden, Ontario (house)

January 25 — Aileen and Pete Pajunen, White River, Ontario (house)

January 26 — Lakehead Motors (Chrysler) parking lot, Thunder Bay, Ontario (camper)

January 27 — Terry Fox Monument parking lot, Thunder Bay, Ontario (camper)

January 28-30 — Lakehead Motors (Chrysler) parking lot, Thunder Bay, Ontario (camper)

January 31-February 1 — Upsala Bible Centre (West Farm), Upsala, Ontario (camper)

February 2 — Buster's Family Restaurant parking lot, Vermilion Bay, Ontario (camper)

February 3-9 — Ken and Sherri Gigliotti and children, Winnipeg, Manitoba (house)

February 10 — Burton Penner, Vermilion Bay, Ontario (camper)

February 11 — Burton Penner, Vermilion Bay, Ontario (cabin)

February 12-13 — Burton Penner, Vermilion Bay, Ontario (camper)

February 14-16 — Ken and Sherri Gigliotti and family, Winnipeg, Manitoba (house)

February 17-March 2 — Flew to Toronto then drove to Washington, D.C., to seeDeclan Haun for last time; he died a week later

March 3 — Bob Diemert, Carman, Manitoba (camper)

March 4 — John and Edith Reimer, Lowe Farm, Manitoba (camper)

March 5 — A and L Drive Inn + Restaurant parking lot, Swan Lake, Manitoba (camper)

March 6 — Red's Cafe parking lot, Wawanesa, Manitoba (camper)

March 7 — Esso gas station parking lot, Souris, Manitoba (camper)

March 8 — A and M Family Food Store parking lot, Redvers, Saskatchewan (camper)

March 9 — Holly's Summer Delight (fruit stand) parking lot, Stoughton, Saskatchewan (camper)

March 10-12 — Doug and Verna Linton, White Bear Lake Resort, Saskatchewan (house)

March 13 — Freedom 1 Oil Rig of Williston Wildcatters, near Carlyle, Saskatchewan (camper)

March 14-15 — Kenting 16E Oil Rig of Williston Wildcatters, near Carlyle, Saskatchewan (engineer's shack)

March 16-17 — Kenting 16E Oil Rig of Williston Wildcatter, near Carlyle, Saskatchewan (camper)

March 18 — Skyway Motel and Restaurant parking lot, Carlyle, Saskatchewan (camper)

March 19 — Maher's Electric and Convenience Store parking lot, Arcola, Saskatchewan (camper)

March 20 — Armand McArthur and family, Kisbey, Saskatchewan (house)

March 21 — Behind hockey arena, Ogema Regional Park, Saskatchewan (camper)

March 22 — Behind grain elevators and railroad tracks, Ponteix, Saskatchewan (camper)

March 23-24 — Behind grandstand, Maple Creek Heritage Park, Saskatchewan (camper)

March 25-26— Wayne and Evelyn Perrin and family, Maple Creek, Saskatchewan (camper)

March 27 — Sue and Dave Elliott and children, Maple Creek, Saskatchewan (camper)

March 28 — Jackson Dodge-Chrysler parking lot, Medicine Hat, Alberta (camper)

March 29 — Foremost and District Civic Centre parking lot, Foremost, Alberta (camper)

March 30 — Burdett Centennial Hall parking lot, Burdett, Alberta (camper)

March 31 — Bridge City Chrysler parking lot, Lethbridge, Alberta (camper)

April 1-3 — Daryl and Janet Hogenson and children, Stirling, Alberta (camper)

April 4 — Bridge City Chrysler parking lot, Lethbridge, Alberta (camper)

April 5 — Daryl and Janet Hogenson and children, Stirling, Alberta (camper)

April 6 — Royal Canadian Legion Branch No. 4 parking lot, Lethbridge, Alberta (camper)

April 7-8 — Daryl and Janet Hogenson and children, Stirling, Alberta (camper)

April 9 — Royal Canadian Legion General Branch No. 4 parking lot, Lethbridge, Alberta (camper)

April 10 — Pete Markus, Lethbridge, Alberta (camper)

April 11-13 — Twin Butte Community Hall parking lot, Alberta (camper)

April 14-15 — Jim Anderson, Pincher Creek, Alberta (camper)

April 16 — Crowsnest Pass Sports Complex parking lot, Coleman, Alberta (camper)

April 17 — Bells Welding Ltd. driveway, Lethbridge, Alberta (camper)

April 18 — Crowsnest Pass Sports Complex parking lot, Coleman, Alberta (camper)

April 19 — Chrysler dealership parking lot, Cranbrook, British Columbia (camper)

April 20-22 — Dave Belcham and family, Ashcroft Ranch, British Columbia (camper)

April 23 — Legacy Park, Ashcroft, British Columbia (camper)

April 24 — Daryl Smith, Savona, British Columbia (camper)

April 25 — Kal West Jeep Eagle dealership parking lot, Vernon, British Columbia (camper)

April 26-27 — Shirley and Robert Louis and family, Vernon, British Columbia (camper)

April 28 — Daryl Smith, Savona, British Columbia (camper)

April 29 — Along Fraser Ave. at Hudson Bay St. in Hope, British Columbia (camper)

April 30 — Gord and Deb Garthwaite, Rey Creek Ranch, Merritt, British Columbia (camper)

May 1 — Gravel Pit, Merritt, British Columbia (camper)

May 2 — Douglas Lake Ranch, Douglas Lake, British Columbia (camper)

May 3 — Shirley and Robert Louis and family, Vernon, British Columbia (camper)

May 4 — Kal West Jeep Eagle dealership parking lot, Vernon, British Columbia (camper)

May 5 — Vancouver ferry dock along slip, British Columbia (camper)

May 6-7 — Wille Dodge parking lot, Victoria, British Columbia (camper)

May 8 — Sealand Market Oceanarium parking lot, Nanaimo, British Columbia (camper)

May 9 — Shell service station parking lot, Port Alberni, British Columbia (camper)

May 10 — Ucluelet dock parking lot, British Columbia (camper)

May 11 — Horseshoe Bay ferry employee parking lot, West Vancouver, British Columbia (camper)

May 12 — Vancouver airport long-term parking lot, Richmond, British Columbia (camper)

May 13 — Frank Vena's apartment on 27th Street, North Vancouver, British Columbia (camper)

May 14 — Gravel Pit, Merritt, British Columbia (camper)

May 15 — Shopping complex parking lot, Kelowna, British Columbia (camper)

May 16-17 — Shirley and Robert Louis, Vernon, British Columbia (camper)

May 18 — CP Rail Yard Storage Tracks parking lot, Spences Bridge, British Columbia (aboard grinding train)

May 19 — CP Rail Yard Storage Tracks parking lot, Spences Bridge, British Columbia (camper)

May 20 — Curling rink parking lot, Falkland, British Columbia (camper)

May 21 — George and Grace Hennessy, Falkland, British Columbia (camper)

May 22 — Falkland Motel parking lot, British Columbia (camper)

May 23 — Shirley and Robert Louis, Vernon, British Columbia (camper)

May 24 — Petro-Canada Travel Centre, Kamloops, British Columbia (camper)

May 25-26 — Shopping mall parking lot, 100 Mile House, British Columbia (camper)

May 27 — In front of library, Clinton, British Columbia (camper)

May 28 — May Ball Rodeo Grounds, Clinton, British Columbia (camper)

May 29 — Shopping mall parking lot, 100 Mile House, British Columbia (camper)

May 30 — Tony Whincup, Soda Creek Emporium, Williams Lake, British Columbia (camper)

May 31-June 1 — Northland Plymouth Chrysler Ltd., Prince George, British Columbia (camper)

June 2 — Mike Broadbent Petro-Canada parking lot, Fort Fraser, British Columbia (camper)

June 3-5 — Kispiox Valley Community Rodeo Grounds, British Columbia (camper)

June 6-8 — Cathy and Dennis, Jesse and Heath Morgan, Terrace, British Columbia (house)

June 9 — Cowbay Harbour parking lot, Prince Rupert, British Columbia (camper)

June 10 — Canadian Legion Hall parking lot, Prince Rupert, British Columbia (camper)

June 11 — Cowbay Harbour parking lot, Prince Rupert, British Columbia (camper)

June 12 — North Pacific Cannery parking lot, Point Edward, British Columbia (camper)

June 13 — Prince Rupert to Skidegate (Queen Charlotte Islands) ferry, British Columbia (camper)

June 14 — Gordon Brown, Masset, Queen Charlotte Islands, British Columbia (camper)

June 15 — Singing Surf Inn parking lot, Masset, Queen Charlotte Islands, British Columbia (camper)

June 16-17 — Campsite off logging road on west shore, Queen Charlotte City, Queen Charlotte Islands, British Columbia (camper)

June 18 — In front of Ross Dixon's home, Old Masset, Queen Charlotte Islands, British Columbia (camper)

June 19-20 — Campsite off logging road on west shore, Queen Charlotte City, Queen Charlotte Islands, British Columbia (camper)

June 21 — Parking lot behind Mary Kelly's home, Queen Charlotte City, British Columbia (camper)

June 22-23 — Skedans Watchmen's camp, Charlie and Caroline Wesley, Queen Charlotte Islands, British Columbia (storage shed)

June 24 — Campsite off logging road on west shore of Kagan Bay, Queen Charlotte Islands, British Columbia (camper)

June 25 — Sandspit Lions Community Centre parking lot, Moresby Island, British Columbia (camper)

June 26-29 — Campsite off logging road on west shore of Kagan Bay, Queen Charlotte Islands, British Columbia (camper)

June 30 — Just off beach at Tow Hill Reserve , Queen Charlotte Islands, British Columbia (camper)

July 1 — Wilfred Penker, Masset, Queen Charlotte Islands, British Columbia (house)

July 2 — Driveway of Alex Rinfret and Don Hancock, Port Clements, Queen Charlotte Islands, British Columbia (camper)

July 3 — Parking lot, Queen Charlotte City, Queen Charlotte Islands, British Columbia (camper)

July 4 — North Pacific Cannery parking lot, Point Edward, British Columbia (camper)

July 5 -6 — Safeway parking lot, Prince Rupert, British Columbia (camper)

July 7 — Cathy, Dennis, Jesse and Heath Morgan, Kitwanga, British Columbia (house)

July 8 — Gitanyow Revival Centre parking lot, Kitwancool, British Columbia (camper)

July 9 — Cathy, Dennis, Jesse and Heath Morgan, Kitwanga, British Columbia (house)

July 10 — Kitwancool Pentecostal Church parking lot, Kitwancool, British Columbia (camper)

July 11 — Bear Glacier rest stop along Hwy 37A, British Columbia (camper)

July 12 — Tahltan Reserve Six Mile fish camp along Stikine River, Telegraph Creek, British Columbia (camper)

July 13 — Parking area at lookout stop on top of Mount Meehaus in Stikine River Recreation Area, British Columbia (camper)

July 14 — Parking area along Cottonwood River on Hwy 37 between Dease Lake and Good Hope Lake, British Columbia (camper)

July 15-20 — David, Rachel and Sterling Ryan, Whitehorse, Yukon Territory (camper)

July 21 — Mike Thomas and Cindy Desaulniers, Whitehorse, Yukon Territory (camper)

July 22-26 — Front street parking, Dawson City, Yukon Territory (camper)

July 27 — Michel Vincent and Grace Jackson, Dawson City, Yukon Territory (camper)

July 28 — Mooseside Gathering, north of Dawson City, Yukon Territory (Phil Gatensby's tent)

July 29 — Drove all night (no sleep) in the land of the midnight sun to Inuvik, Northwest Territories

July 30-August 2 — Osman Daoud, Inuvik, Northwest Territories (house)

August 3 — (Flew to Tuktoyaktuk) Behind the House of Hope, Tuktoyaktuk, Northwest Territories (tent, borrowed from Osman Daoud)

August 4 — Willie and Alice Carpenter's family summer camp tent, Tuktoyaktuk, Northwest Territories

August 5-7 — Bob and Jean Grubin's family cabin, Tuktoyaktuk, Northwest Territories

August 8-10 — Bob and Jean Grubin's home, Tuktoyaktuk, Northwest Territories

August 11-12 — (Flew back to Inuvik) Osman Daoud, Inuvik, Northwest Territories (house)

August 13 — Deadend of Lagoon Road, Inuvik, Northwest Territories (camper)

August 14 — Rocky's Plumbing and Heating parking lot, Inuvik, Northwest Territories (camper)

August 15 — Deadend of Lagoon Road, Inuvik, Northwest Territories (camper)

August 16-18 — Eddie Dean Kolausok, Inuvik, Northwest Territories (camper)

August 19-21 — (Flew to Yellowknife to photograph the Queen's visit) Diane Taylor, Yellowknife, Northwest Territories (house)

August 22 — (Flew to Rankin Inlet to photograph the Queen's visit) Siniktarvik Hotel, Northwest Territories (stayed with Peter Jones of Reuters and Alain Buu of Gamma Liason)

August 23-25 — A. E., Rankin Inlet, Northwest Territories (house)

August 26 — Pierre Okoktok, Rankin Inlet, Northwest Territories (house)

August 27-29 — Laurel Ratsoy and Anne Sholod, "the barn" (nurses' residence), Rankin Inlet, Northwest Territories

August 30 — (Flew back to Yellowknife) Diane Taylor, Yellowknife, Northwest Territories (house)

August 31 — (Flew back to Inuvik) Eddie Dean Kolausok, Inuvik, Northwest Territories (camper)

September 1 — Beside Visitor Centre in Inuvik, Northwest Territories (camper)

September 2 — Eagle Plains parking lot, Dempster Highway, Yukon Territory (camper)

September 3-4 — Michel Vincent and Grace Jackson, Dawson City, Yukon Territory (camper)

September 5 — Carmacks motel parking lot, Yukon Territory (camper)

September 6 — David, Rachel and Sterling Ryan, Whitehorse, Yukon Territory (camper)

September 7-8 — Metro Chrysler Ltd., Whitehorse, Yukon Territory (camper)

September 9-10 — John Hutch, "Photographic John," Moccasin Flats, Whitehorse, Yukon Territory (camper)

September 11-12 — Doug Smarch Jr., Whitehorse, Yukon Territory (camper)

September 13 — Atlin wharf, British Columbia (camper)

September 14-16 — Gernot Dick, Atlin Art Centre, British Columbia (camper)

September 17 — Petro-Canada along Alaska hwy, (camper)

September 18 — Belvedere Motor Hotel parking lot, Watson Lake, Yukon Territory (camper)

September 19-20 — Liard Hot Springs parking lot, British Columbia (camper)

September 21 — Buckinghorse River Provincial Park parking lot, British Columbia (camper)

September 22 — Open (24) Hours truck stop parking lot, Whitecourt, Alberta (camper)

September 23 — Tourism Centre parking lot on Hwy 2, Edmonton, Alberta (camper)

September 24 — Galloway (train) Station Museum parking lot, Edson, Alberta(camper)

September 25 — Public parking lot beside railroad, Jasper, Alberta (camper)

September 26 — Lake Louise Samson Mall parking lot, Lake Louise, Alberta (camper)

September 27 — Banff Springs Hotel parking lot, Alberta (camper)

September 28-29 — Todd and Tracey Korol, Calgary, Alberta (house)

September 30 — Shopping mall parking lot, Calgary, Alberta (camper)

October 1-2 — Memorial Arena parking lot, Drumheller, Alberta (camper)

October 3 — Recreational Park parking lot, Alliance, Alberta (camper)

October 4 — Holy Heart of Mary Catholic Church parking lot, Viking, Alberta (camper)

October 5 — Chrysler dealership in Camrose, Alberta (camper)

October 6 — Tourism Centre parking lot on Hwy 2, Edmonton, Alberta (camper)

October 7 — In front of Mission Church, Beaver Mines, Alberta (camper)

October 8-9 — Sorting pens parking lot for Pincher Creek Stockmens Association in Bow Crow Forest, Alberta (camper)

October 10-11 — Todd and Tracey Korol, Calgary, Alberta (house)

October 12-13 — Twin Butte Community Hall parking lot, Alberta (camper)

October 14 — Wayne and Evelyn Perrin and family, Maple Creek, Saskatchewan (camper)

October 15 — Ranger's Station, Cypress Hills Interprovincial Park, West Block, Saskatchewan (camper)

October 16 — Trailor drop-off parking lot, Cypress Hills Interprovincial Park, West Block, Saskatchewan (camper)

October 17 — Frank and Donna Nuttall, Maple Creek, Saskatchewan (camper)

October 18 — Richard and Joyce Nuttal, Maple Creek, Saskatchewan (camper)

October 19 — Bridge City Chrysler parking lot, Lethbridge, Alberta (camper)

October 20 — Royal Canadian Legion Branch No. 4 parking lot, Lethbridge, Alberta (camper)

October 21 — Head Smashed in Buffalo Jump overflow parking lot, Alberta (camper)

October 22-23 — Greg and Tami Delinte, Lower Waldron Ranch, Alberta (house)

October 24 — Greg and Tami Delinte, Lower Waldron Ranch, Alberta (camper)

October 25-26 — Lundbreck Community Hall, Alberta (camper)

October 27 — Bridge City Chrysler parking lot, Lethbridge, Alberta (camper)

October 28 — Alberta Sugar Corporation parking lot, Taber, Alberta (camper)

October 29-30 — Sparrow Gardens hockey arena parking lot, Caronport, Saskatchewan (camper)

October 31 — In front of Richard Marjan's home, Saskatoon, Saskatchewan (camper)

November 1-2 — Sparrow Gardens hockey arena parking lot, Caronport, Saskatchewan (camper)

November 3 — CFB Moosejaw parking lot, Saskatchewan (camper)

November 4-6 — Sparrow Gardens hockey arena parking lot, Caronport, Saskatchewan (camper)

November 7-8 — In front of Richard Marjan's home, Saskatoon, Saskatchewan (camper)

November 9 — Armand and Bev McArthur and family, Kisbey, Saskatchewan (camper)

November 10 — Campground of Lions Community Park, Carlyle, Saskatchewan (camper)

November 11-14 — Audrey and Howard Young, Carlyle, Saskatchewan (camper)

November 15 — Armand and Bev McArthur and family, Kisbey, Saskatchewan (camper)

November 16 — Indian Head Chrysler parking lot, Saskatchewan (camper)

November 17 — G and E Family Restaurant parking lot, Foam Lake, Saskatchewan (camper)

November 18 — In front of Sports Complex in Canora Community Park, Saskatchewan (camper)

November 19-20 — Crestview Dodge parking lot, Regina, Saskatchewan (camper)

November 21-22 — In front of Richard Marjan's home, Saskatoon, Saskatchewan (camper)

November 23 — The Harbour Inn parking lot, La Ronge, Saskatchewan (camper)

November 24-25 — Waterbase Inn parking lot, La Ronge, Saskatchewan (camper)

November 26 — Scott and Karen Robertson, Air Ronge, Saskatchewan (house)

November 27-29 — Waterbase Inn parking lot, La Ronge, Saskatchewan (camper)

November 30-December 2 — Simon Eninew's camp, Gow Lake, Saskatchewan (cabin)

December 3 — Waterbase Inn, La Ronge parking lot, Saskatchewan (camper)

December 4-6 — Jocelyn Cook, Stanley Mission, Saskatchewan (house)

December 7-11 — Roy Isbister, Susie Bird and Lorraine Cook, La Ronge, Saskatchewan (house)

December 12-14 — Greenstone Community Futures Development Corporation parking lot, Flin Flon, Manitoba (camper)

December 15-16 — Flin Flon Friendship Centre, Manitoba (room)

December 17-19 — Roy Isbister, Susie Bird and Lorraine Cook, La Ronge, Saskatchewan (house)

December 20 — Dawson Bay Hotel parking lot, Mafeking, Manitoba (camper)

December 21 — Petro-Canada parking lot, Minnedosa, Manitoba (camper)

December 22 — Burton and Carlyn Penner and family, Vermilion Bay, Ontario (camper)

December 23 — Gary and Judy Boissineau and family, Heyden, Ontario (camper)

End of Journey (for now)

ABOARD A FERRY FROM THE QUEEN CHARLOTTE ISLANDS
TO PRINCE RUPERT, BRITISH COLUMBIA
All across Canada, on land or sea, the horizon beckons travellers on
and defines a corner of the world for those who live there.
Whether you're passing through or staying put, it's comforting and
welcoming — part of being home.